I BELIE

By Dr. J. Eldon Neihof, Sr.

I Believe in Holiness
By Dr. J. Eldon Neihof, Sr.

Perfect Bound
ISBN 978-1-60416-42-2
Trade Cloth
ISBN 978-1-60416-43-8

Printed On Demand

Reformation Publishers
242 University Drive
Prestonsburg, KY 41653
1-800-765-2464
Fax 606-886-8222
rpublisher@aol.com
www.reformationpublishers.com

Printed and bound in the United States of America

Foreword

"I am sure that you will be challenged by the plain, logical writings of Dr. J. Eldon Neihof, Sr. Dad has a gift to communicate the holiness message clearly and simply. I have never questioned the reality of the experience of second blessing holiness, because I saw it credibly, consistently, and faithfully modeled before me in my dad. "Throughout the holiness movement, Dad is honored as a clear exponent and a living example of the beauty of holiness. His chapter, <u>Why I Believe in Holiness</u>, remains one of my favorites. This book will challenge you to go deeper with God. The call to holiness rings clearly throughout its pages.
"I am pleased to present to you my priest, my teacher, my example, my theologian, my favorite preacher... my dad."

John E. Neihof, Jr., Ph.D.

Contents

Introduction

When I was fifteen years of age, I felt definitely that God called me to preach the Gospel. I was first saved at age eight. I was unsettled in my relationship with the Lord during my early teens and was back and forth to the altar many times. In my seventeenth year the Lord led me into the experience of heart holiness. It was after I made a full surrender to Jesus Christ and was entirely sanctified that I began to grow spiritually, and I began to have a settled, consistent walk with the Lord.

I was privileged to attend Mt. Carmel High School and Kentucky Mountain Bible Institute (now College). I had wonderful instructors regarding the way of Scriptural holiness. I was privileged to attend Asbury College and many holiness camp meetings where I heard many of the great holiness preachers of that time.

The message of holiness began to burn in my heart. Over the years I began to realize that holiness was not being preached in many places. I increasingly felt the need of proclaiming this Scriptural truth.

As I have preached in revivals and camp meetings, increasingly people have asked if I had any of my messages in print. I do not consider myself a writer and realize that many greater than I have proclaimed this message both in pulpit and in print.

As I prayed about it, I felt the Lord would have me put some of my messages in print on the subject of holiness. I pray that these messages will be all for the glory of God and the help of many in the way of Scriptural holiness.

I want to express my sincere thanks to my dear wife who has proofed my writing and has been my beloved companion and encourager as I have endeavored to proclaim the holiness message.

Why I Believe In Holiness

"But sanctify the Lord God in your hearts: and be ready always to give an answer to every man that asketh you a reason of the hope that is in you with meekness and fear" (I Peter 3:15).

I begin with a question. This is the question. Why do I believe in holiness? Is it because it is the doctrine of my church? Is it because my parents believe in it? Is it because it's what I was taught in school? Why do I believe in holiness?

I want to suggest five reasons the Lord has given me as to why I believe in holiness.

First of all, I believe in holiness because of the problem of sin. The Bible makes it clear that sin is a two-fold problem. There is the practice of sin and there is the principle of sin. There is the act of sin, and there is the inner polluted nature of sin. There are sins committed, and there is sin inherited.

Stealing is the practice of sin, and covetousness is the underlying principle. The commandment says, "Thou shalt not steal" (Exodus 20:15). Another commandment says, "Thou shalt not covet" (Exodus 20:17). One may covet and not steal, but no one steals without first coveting. You can be forgiven for the stealing, but a cleansing is needed to deal with the covetous principle in the heart that prompted the act of stealing.

Lying is the practice of sin, while deceit is the principle cause. The command says, "Thou shalt not bear false witness" (Exodus 20:16). Jeremiah tells us that "The heart is deceitful above all things, and desperately wicked: who can know it?" (Jeremiah 17:9). The dishonest person can be forgiven, but a cleansing is needed to deal with the deceitful nature within the heart that prompted the dishonesty.

We recognize murder as the practice of sin while hate, revenge, malice and anger may well be the inner underlying cause that prompted the act of murder. The command says, "Thou shalt not kill" (Exodus 20:13). John writes in I John 3:15 and says, "Whosoever hateth his brother is a murderer."

We know that the murderer can be forgiven for the act of murder, but a cleansing is needed to deal with the hate, revenge, malice and anger that may very well have provoked the murderous act.

Adultery is the practice of sin while lust is the underlying principle. The commandment says, "Thou shalt not commit adultery." Jesus said, "Whosoever looketh on a woman to lust after her hath committed adultery with her already in his heart" (Matthew 5:28). The adulterer or adulteress can be forgiven, but a cleansing is needed to deal with the principle of lust that provoked the sinful act.

The Apostle Paul distinguished between "sins" and "sin" in his letter to the Roman church. In Romans 3:23 he says, "All have sinned and come short of the glory of God." This clearly refers to the practice of sin. In Romans 5:8 Paul says, "God commendth His love toward us, in that, while we were yet sinners, Christ died for us." Again, Paul is speaking of the practice of sin and sinning. In Romans 5:12 he says, "Wherefore, as by one man (Adam) sin (the sinful nature) entered into the world, and death by sin (the sinful nature) and so death passed upon all men, for that all have sinned (as a sinful practice)." Adam Clark said, "All are born with a sinful nature, and the seeds of this evil soon bring forth corresponding fruit." In Romans 6:1 Paul asks a question. He says, "Shall we continue in sin that grace may abound?" He answers the question in verse two and says, "God forbid" or by no means. In verse fourteen he says, "For sin (the sinful nature) shall not have dominion over you. In verse twenty-two he says, "But now being made free from sin (both the act of sin and the sinful nature), and become servants to God, ye have your fruit unto holiness, and the end everlasting life".

Having voluntarily transgressed God's law man needs to repent and be pardoned by faith in Jesus Christ. Having involuntarily been born with a depraved sinful nature man needs to be cleansed from inherited sin in a second work of grace, called entire sanctification, likewise received by faith.

Inherited sin is the cause, while outward sin is the effect. Inherited sin is the root of the sin problem, while outward sin is the fruit. Jesus said, "For from within, out of the heart of men, proceed evil thoughts, adulteries, fornications, murders, thefts, covetousness, wickedness, deceit, lasciviousness, an evil eye, blasphemy, pride, foolishness: all these evil things come from within and defile the man" (Mark 7:21-23). Dr. Paul Rees said, "When you read these verses it sounds like you're reading a sewer inspector's report."

A man is a sinner because he practices sin. He sins because he is sinful in his heart and nature. Behind the doing of sin is the being of sin, and it is only by removing the cause that the effect will cease. Forgiveness is for our wrong doing. Cleansing is for our wrong being. I heard Bother Paul Hill say, "The heart of the trouble is the trouble of the heart."

I believe in holiness because sin is a two-fold problem and requires a two-fold remedy. We need forgiveness for sins committed, and we need cleansing for sin inherited.

A second reason I believe in holiness is because of the provisions of Christ. John tells us that Christ was manifested for a two-fold purpose. In I John 3:5 he says that He (Christ) was manifested to take away our sins. In I John 3:8 John says, "For this purpose the Son of God was manifested, that He might destroy the works of the devil." Verse five reminds me of the Old Testament scape goat. The priest would lay his hands on the head of that animal and confess the sins of the people. The animal would then be released to wander in the wilderness, typifying the taking away of their sins. John says Jesus was manifested to take away our sins. He became our scapegoat. "Who His own self bare our sins in His own body on the tree, that we, being dead to sins should live unto righteousness ..." (I Peter 2:24). John says Jesus was manifested not only to take away our sins but to destroy the works of the devil. The carnal mind is not the devil in the heart of man, but it is certainly the devil's work. What greater work could Satan have done than to infect the whole human race with the nature of sin. Every baby born into this world is born with a sinful nature so that we do not have to teach them to do wrong. They do wrong because of the pollution of sin in the heart that is bent in that direction. John says Jesus was manifested to destroy that sinful nature in man's heart. Paul writes in Romans 6:6 "Knowing this, that our old man (the carnal mind) is crucified (put to death) with Him, that the body of sin (the carnal mind) might be destroyed (not suppressed), that henceforth we should not serve sin (be slaves to the carnal mind)."

There are two objectives of Christ's death: the saving of sinners and the sanctification of believers. "God commended His love toward us, in that, while we were yet sinners, Christ died for us" (Romans 5:8). "Wherefore, Jesus also, that He might sanctify the people with His own blood, suffered without the gate" (Hebrews 13:12).

There are two expressions of Divine love. God's love for sinners and Christ's love for the church. "For God so loved the world, that He gave His only begotten Son, that whosoever believeth in Him should not perish, but have everlasting life" (John 3:16). "The Lord is not slack concerning His promise, as some men count slackness; but is longsuffering to us-ward, not willing that any should perish, but that all should come to repentance" (II Peter 3:9). "...Christ also loved the church, and gave Himself for it; that He might sanctify and cleanse it with the washing of water by the word, that He might present it to Himself a glorious church, not having spot, or wrinkle, or any such thing; but that it should be holy and without blemish" (Ephesians 5:25-27).

There are two prayers of Jesus. The first is for sinners, and the second is for believers. Jesus was on the cross, and He prayed for those that crucified Him and for all sinners. "Then said Jesus, Father forgive them; for they know not what they do" (Luke 23:34). In John 17:17, Jesus prayed for His disciples. He said, "Sanctify them through Thy truth: Thy word is truth." In John 17:20 He said, "Neither pray I for these (disciples) alone, but for them also which shall believe on me through their word." This includes all believers. He prayed that all born again Christians might be sanctified.

There are two great experiences wrought by the Holy Spirit. There is the birth of the Spirit and the baptism of the Spirit.

Jesus said in John 3:5 "...Except a man be born of water and of the Spirit he cannot enter into the kingdom of God." John the Baptist said in Matthew 3:11, "I indeed baptize you with water unto repentance: but He that cometh after me is mightier than I, whose shoes I am not worthy to bear: He shall baptize you with the Holy Ghost and with fire."

There are two Divine requirements set forth in the Scripture. They are the confession of sin for pardon and walking in light for cleansing. "If we confess our sins, He is faithful and just to forgive us our sins, and to cleanse us from all unrighteousness" (I John 1:9). In I John 1:7 John said, "But if we walk in the light, as He is in the light, we have fellowship one with another, and the blood of Jesus Christ His Son cleanseth us from all sin."

It has been said that "The minimum of the atonement must cover the maximum of the fall. If there is no double cure for sin, there is no adequate cure."

> "Rock of ages, cleft for me,
> Let me hide myself in Thee.
> Let the water and the blood,
> From Thy wounded side which flowed,
> Be of sin the double cure,
> Save from wrath and make me pure."

I believe in holiness because of the provisions of Christ.

Thirdly, I believe in holiness because of the plain teaching of the Bible.

The Bible teaches that holiness is God's choice for man from all eternity. The Apostle Paul stated in Ephesians 1:4, "According as He hath chosen us in Him before the foundation of the world, that we should be holy and without blame before Him in love."

The Bible teaches that holiness is God's will. Paul wrote to the Christians at Thessalonica and said in I Thessalonians 4:3, "For this is the will of God, even your sanctification, that ye should abstain from fornication." Paul was saying to believers that if they were going to be established in their faith and kept from going back to their old heathen ways they would need to get sanctified.

The Bible teaches that holiness is God's call. "For God hath not called us unto uncleanness, but unto holiness" (I Thessalonians 4:7).

The Bible teaches us that holiness is God's command. Peter said in I Peter 1:15-16, "But as He which hath called you is holy, so be ye holy in all manner of conversation (life style); because it is written, be ye holy; for I am holy."

The Bible teaches that holiness is the Christian's inheritance (birthright). In Acts 20:32 we read, "And now, brethren, I commend you to God, and to the word of His grace, which is able to build you up, and to give you an inheritance among all them which are sanctified."

The Bible teaches that holiness is required for heaven. The Psalmist said in Psalm 24:3-4 "Who shall ascend into the hill of the Lord? Or who shall stand in His holy place? He that hath clean hands and a pure heart; who hath not lifted up his soul unto vanity, nor sworn deceitfully." The Hebrew writer states in Hebrews 12:14, "Follow peace with all men, and holiness, without which no man shall see the Lord."

Holiness is the great theme of the Bible. God was and is in the business of preparing a holy people for Himself.

I believe in holiness because of the plain teachings of God's Word.

Fourthly, I believe in holiness because of the people that have witnessed to it.

Go back to the Old Testament. We have the Bible character Jacob. He had two crisis experiences with God that changed his life. The first was at Bethel, and the second was at Peniel. When he came to Bethel he was fleeing from his brother Esau. Jacob had tricked him out of his birthright and blessing. Esau said, "If I get my hands on Jacob, I'll kill him." Jacob fled for his life. At Bethel he slept on a pile of rocks. He dreamed of a ladder reaching from earth to heaven. Angels were ascending and descending. When he awoke he said in Genesis 28:16, "Surely the Lord is in this place and I knew it not." In Genesis 28: 21-22 he said, "...Then shall the Lord be my God ....Of all that Thou shalt give me I will surely give the tenth unto Thee." He had a life changing encounter with God at Bethel. He journeyed on to uncle Laban's. He married, had a family and acquired great wealth which was measured by the size of his herd of cattle. He felt it was time to return to Canaan. He started his journey. He had not gone far until a servant informed him that Esau was coming to meet him with four hundred men. He was fearful for he remembered the last word he had from Esau.. He said,"When I see Jacob I'll kill him." Jacob came to the brook, Jabbok. He sent his cattle across the brook. He sent his servants and his wives and children across the brook. Jacob stayed and wrestled with an angel. His name and nature were changed. He was no longer Jacob, trickster, or deceiver. He became Israel, a prince with God.

David prayed for pardon and cleansing in (Psalm 51:2,5,7,10). He said, "Wash me throughly from mine iniquity, and cleanse me from my sin. Behold I was shapen in iniquity, and in sin did my mother conceive me. Purge me with hyssop, and I shall be clean: wash me, and I shall be whiter than snow. Create in me a clean heart, O God, and renew a right spirit within me."

Isaiah prayed for cleansing in Isaiah 6:5. He said, "Woe is me, for I am undone; because I am a man of unclean lips, and I dwell in the midst of a people of unclean lips: for mine eyes have seen the King, the Lord of Hosts." It was then that God sent a seraphim with a live coal from the altar of God to touch his lips. His iniquity was taken away, and his sin purged.

We come to the New Testament. The book of Acts records six cases where believers received the Holy Spirit in a second work of grace. They are found in Acts 2,8,9,10,18 and 19. In Acts 2 we read of the Jerusalem Pentecost where one hundred twenty believers were baptized with the Holy Spirit. In Act 8 Philip went to Samaria and had a revival. Many were converted. They sent for Peter and John. They came and laid hands on these new believers and they received the baptism of the Holy Spirit. In Acts 9 we have the record of the conversion of the Apostle Paul. This was followed by his going to Damascus. Under the influence and ministry of godly Ananias he received the baptism with the Holy Spirit. In Acts 10 we have the Gentile Pentecost at the house of Cornelius. Peter testified in Acts 15:8-9, "And God, which knoweth the hearts, bare them (Gentiles) witness, giving them the Holy Ghost, even as He did unto us (Jews); and put no difference between us and them, purifying their hearts by faith." In Acts 18 we find a young evangelist by the name of Apollos. He knew only the baptism of John. A Spirit-filled couple, Aquilla and Priscilla, took him and taught him the things of God more perfectly. In Act 19 the Apostle Paul arrives at Ephesus on his third missionary journey. His first question to these believers was, "Have ye received the Holy Ghost since ye believed?" Their answer was in the negative. Under Paul's ministry they received the baptism of the Holy Spirit.

The Apostle Paul emphasized this truth to all his churches. The Corinthian church was carnal and needed heart purity and the fullness of the Spirit. To the Thessalonian Christians he said in, I Thessalonians 5:23, "The very God of peace sanctify you wholly; and I pray God your whole spirit and soul and body be preserved blameless unto the coming of our Lord Jesus Christ."

John Wesley witnessed to heart holiness. He said, "Many years since I say that without holiness no man shall see the Lord. I began following after it and inciting all with whom I had any contact to do the same. Ten years after, God gave me a clearer view than ever before of the way to attain this: namely by faith in the Son of God. And immediately I declared to all, we are made holy by faith. This I testified in private, public, in print, and God confirmed it by a thousand witnesses. I have continued to confirm this for about thirty years."

John Fletcher, a contemporary of John Wesley, bore clear witness to heart holiness. Adam Clark, the writer of the commentary bearing his name, gave witness to entire sanctification as a second work of grace. These are people I never knew but have been blessed to read after. There are many others among them such as Bishop Asbury of early Methodism, Dr. Daniel Steele, Alfred Cookman, John Inskip, Samuel Logan Brengle, W. B. Godbey, Henry Clay Morrison, Bud Robinson, C. W. Ruth and many more.

There are many other witnesses that I have known personally. Aunt Lucy Henderson from my home area in northern Kentucky was a sanctified saint of God. Her life and testimony impressed me deeply. Rev. H. J. Hervey was my pastor as a boy. I was converted under his ministry. He proclaimed this message of scriptural holiness. I came to Mt. Carmel High School and the Kentucky Mountain Bible Institute (now College). I was influenced by Dr. Lela G McConnell, Miss Martha Archer, Dr. Karl Paulo and others. I was privileged to attend many holiness camp meetings and heard great holiness preachers such as Dr. Paul Rees, Dr. Tony Anderson, Dr. Roy Nicholson, Dr. Lawrence Hicks, Dr. Richard Taylor, Rev. Joshua Stauffer, Rev. C. L. Thompson and many more of God's choice servants.

One of the strongest testimonies that touched my life was that of a fellow student in high school. This young man had a terrible temper. He was dismissed from school for fighting. He had a godly mother. She brought her son back to school and talked with Dr. McConnell, the president. She said, "I'm praying for God to make a holiness preacher out of my son. Will you give him another chance and let him come back to school?" He was allowed to return to school on condition he would not fight or tell the teachers off. He signed the agreement and returned to school. He was not there long until he realized he had made a hard agreement to live by. He came to the principal and said, "I'm not interested in being a Christian. I just don't want to get kicked out of school." The principal said, "You have an uncontrollable temper. Your only hope is the grace of God." He left, not liking what he heard. Later he returned, repented and got gloriously saved. He went on to make a total surrender to God's will and experienced God's sanctifying grace in his life. He was a challenge to every student to be completely sold out to Jesus Christ. God called him to preach and has given him a great ministry winning souls and leading others into the blessing of heart holiness.

I believe in holiness because of the many that have witnessed to it.

Fifthly, I believe in holiness because of personal experience.

This is my strongest reason. Men can gainsay your logic and theology, but they cannot gainsay what God has done in your heart and life.

I was first saved in a revival meeting in my home church at the age of eight years. I was hungry for God and can never remember being rebellious. I was very weak and was back and forth at the altar many times as a child and also in my teen years. I attended Mt. Carmel Christian High School and sought the Lord the first day on campus. I heard entire sanctification preached, sought it and professed it. However, I continued to be very unstable in my Christian walk. In my junior year of high school I experienced another spiritual failure. I was very discouraged. I longed to have a consistent walk with God. On March 8, 1952, the Lord reclaimed me and brought peace and assurance to my heart that my sins were forgiven. The next day was Sunday. I went to church with the express purpose of being a seeker for heart holiness. The Apostle Paul said in Romans 5:1,2 "Therefore being justified by faith, we have peace with God through our Lord Jesus Christ: by whom also we have access by faith into this grace wherein we stand, and rejoice in hope of the glory of God." I needed that grace that would enable me to stand. I was convinced that the reason I had been so unstable in my Christian life was the fact I had never truly been sanctified. When the altar call was given I responded without hesitation. That day I made a complete surrender of my life to Jesus Christ. The witness came to my heart that the blood did indeed cleanse from all sin. Surrendering my life to Jesus Christ was the smartest thing I ever did. That experience has made all the difference in my life. That crisis experience has been followed by a process of growth and development in the sanctified life. There is both an altar work and an after work.

In August of 1957, I traveled to Texas to lead singing in a revival meeting. The first night of the meeting I sat on the front bench selecting songs when the evangelist, who happened to be the pastor, sat down beside me and said, "I'm not a second blessing holiness man." I answered and said, "I am and would like to be free to sing about it, pray about it and testify to it while I'm here." He said, "That's fine. My mother believes in it. My wife believes in it, but I've never been able to see it." It was not an easy meeting but God helped me in a wonderful way.

It was in my motel room during that meeting that this question came to my mind, why do I believe in holiness? God spoke to me that day and I came to this conclusion. I believe in holiness:

   I. Because of the problem of sin

  II. Because of the provisions of Christ

 III. Because of the plain teachings of the Bible

 IV. Because of the people that have witnessed to it

  V. Because of personal experience

The Carnal Mind

Romans 8:1-9

The Bible teaches that man is born innocent before God, but at the same time he is born with a corrupt sinful nature. David said, "Behold, I was shapen in iniquity; and in sin did my mother conceive me" (Psalm 51:5). The Apostle Paul said, "We are by nature the children of wrath" (Ephesians 2:3). Both David and Paul agree that we were born with a depraved sinful nature.

The Bible teaches that this corrupt nature remains in the heart of the believer after conversion. From the apostles until now the church in general has confirmed this teaching. One church states: "We believe that original sin, or depravity, is that corruption of nature of all the offspring of Adam, by reason of which everyone is very far gone from original righteousness, or the pure state of our first parents at the time of their creation, is averse to God, is without spiritual life, and is inclined to evil, and that continually; and that it continues to exist with the new life of the regenerate."

This evil tendency or proneness to evil is referred to by different names, such as: original sin, the Adamic sin nature, depravity, inbred sin, the law of sin, the sin that dwelleth in me, the body of death, our old man, the flesh, the bent to sin and the carnal mind.

Some believe that the carnal mind is located in the physical body. The Bible teaches that the body is a gift of God and may be used for the glory of God. The Apostle Paul writes in I Corinthians 6:19,20 and says, "What? Know ye not that your body is the temple of the Holy Ghost which is in you, which ye have of God, and ye are not your own? For ye are bought with a price: therefore glorify God in your body, and in your spirit, which are God's." Jesus lived in a human body without sin for thirty-three years. He demonstrated that it is possible to live holy while living in a human body. He further demonstrated that the human body was intended to be God's temple and dwelling place.

The New Testament teaches the body may be presented to God holy. Romans 12:1 says, "I beseech you therefore brethren, by the mercies of God, that ye present your bodies a living sacrifice, holy, acceptable unto God, which is your reasonable service."

The scripture makes it clear that the body may be yielded to God as an instrument of righteousness and holiness. In Romans 6:13 Paul writes, "Neither yield ye your members as instruments of unrighteousness unto sin: but yield yourselves unto God as those that are alive from the dead, and your members as instruments of righteousness unto God." Paul speaks further at this point in Romans 6:19 and says, "I speak after the manner of men because of the infirmity of your flesh: for as ye have (past tense) yielded your members servants to uncleanness and to iniquity unto iniquity; even so now yield your members servants to righteousness unto holiness."

God's Word further declares that the body may be the dwelling place of a holy God. In II Corinthians 6:16 the apostle writes, "Ye are the temple of the living God; as God hath said, I will dwell in them, and walk in them, and I will be their God, and they shall be my people."

Again the Word of God speaks and tells us the body may be preserved blameless unto the coming of Jesus Christ. We read it in I Thessalonians 5:23 where Paul says, "The very God of peace sanctify you wholly (entirely); and I pray God your whole spirit and soul and body be preserved blameless unto the coming of our Lord Jesus Christ."

Christ lived in a human body and seeks to indwell our bodies in the person of the Holy Spirit. He would never dwell where sin dwells. There is nothing sinful about your body. God wants to hallow it with His sanctifying presence.

The Bible teaches that the carnal mind is not located in the body but rather is located in the affections and will of man. Jesus asked in Matthew 12:34, "How can ye, being evil, speak good things? For out of the abundance of the heart the mouth speaketh." The wise man of the Old Testament, Solomon, wrote in Proverbs 4:23 and said, "Keep thy heart with all diligence, for out of it are the issues of life."

Jesus again spoke in Mark 7:21-23, and said, "For from within, out of the heart of men proceed evil thoughts, adulteries, fornications, murders, thefts, covetousness, wickedness, deceit, lasciviousness, an evil eye, blasphemy, pride, foolishness; all these evil things come from within and defile the man." The Apostle Paul writes in Galatians 5:19-21, according to the New International Version, and says, "The acts of the sinful nature are obvious: sexual immorality, impurity and debauchery; idolatry and witchcraft, hatred, discord, jealousy, fits of rage, selfish ambition, dissensions, factions and envy, drunkenness, orgies, and the like. I warn you, as I did before, that those who live like this will not inherit the kingdom of God." Here the carnal mind is likened to a sinful factory that manufactures all sorts of sin and wickedness.

Sin is two-fold. We need forgiveness for sins committed. We need cleansing for sin inherited. Rev. Paul Hill said, "The heart of the trouble is the trouble of the heart."

In Romans 8:8 Paul says, "They that are in the flesh cannot please God." The word flesh as used here does not refer to the physical body. It means so long as we are under the reigning power of the fleshly, sinful, carnal mind we cannot do that which pleases God so long as this state exists, and we continue to be governed by carnal appetites and carnal desires.

The carnal mind is not located in the physical body. It is a matter of the heart, affections and will of man.

The carnal mind is not sin as an act of disobedience. Acts of sin are the fruit. The carnal mind is the root of the sin problem. It is the relationship of the cause to the effect. The carnal mind is the inner cause of the sin problem.

The carnal mind is not normal God given appetites, desires and drives such as hunger, thirst and the desire for the opposite sex. These desires are not sinful or carnal. They are God given desires. It is not wrong to get hungry. It is wrong to steal food to satisfy the hunger. It is not wrong to be attracted to the opposite sex. It is wrong to satisfy that sexual desire outside of marriage. It is the misuse and abuse of these normal God given desires that is wrong.

The carnal mind is not human infirmities such as weariness, forgetfulness and error in judgment. This is humanity affected by the fall. It is not carnality.

Dr. John R. Church said he believed in both eradication and suppression. He believed in the eradication of the carnal and the suppression of the human. He believed in the cleansing of the carnal and the discipline of the human.

Human emotions, drives and desires need to be disciplined and controlled. The Apostle Paul said, "I keep under my body, and bring it into subjection: lest that by any means, when I have preached to others, I myself should be a castaway" (I Corinthians 9:27). I must control my human drives and not let them control me. We must control our appetite for food. If we do not control our appetite we will become obese, damage our health and possibly shorten our lives.

Paul says in Romans 8:6 that, "To be carnally minded is death." The carnal mind is the way to spiritual death and backsliding. Paul wrote to the Thessalonian Christians in I Thessalonians 4:3 and said, "This is the will of God, even your sanctification, that ye should abstain from fornication." These believers had been saved out of heathenism. Fornication or immorality was a part of their heathen life style. Paul believed that if they were going to be kept from going back to their old heathen ways they needed to be cleansed from the carnal mind in entire sanctification. The carnal mind would tend to draw them away from God and lead to spiritual death and backsliding.

Paul says in Romans 8:7 that, "The carnal mind is enmity against God: for it is not subject to the law of God, neither indeed can be." The carnal mind is a rebel nature. It is marked by hostility against God. It is insubordinate. It will not submit. It is self sovereign. It insists on its own way.

In Romans 7:21 Paul speaks of the carnal mind as an evil tendency. He says, "I find then a law, that, when I would do good, evil is present with me." It is similar to the law of gravity. It pulls downward toward sin. Charles Wesley speaks of the carnal mind as a bent to evil in his great hymn, "Love

Divine, All Loves Excelling." The second stanza reads like this, "Breathe, oh, breathe Thy loving Spirit into every troubled breast! Let us all in Thee inherit; let us find that second rest. Take away our bent to sinning; Alpha an Omega be. End of faith, as its beginning, set our hearts at liberty." The carnal mind is a mindedness or a mind set toward the world, self and sin. It is not a thing like a bad tooth that can be extracted. It is a disposition or an inclination away from God and toward evil.

Before Adam sinned, every inclination was to seek God, to walk with God, to fellowship with God, to love God, to serve God and to please God. But when sin entered in the fall of man the inclination was to hide from God, to lie, to cheat, to steal, to murder and to do all sorts of evil. Thus, we see Cain murder his own brother, Abel.

This evil tendency is evident in our children. We don't have to teach them to do wrong. We do have to teach them to do right. We don't have to teach them to lie, cheat or steal. We do have to teach them to tell the truth, to be honest and not to take anything that does not belong to them.

Man has a nature that is bent toward evil. Thus, it becomes as natural to sin as it is for a hog to go to a mud hole, an apple to fall to the ground, a bird to fly, or a duck to swim.

This evil nature is inherited by all. "As by one man (Adam) sin entered into the world and death by sin and so death passed upon all men, for that all have sinned" (Romans 5:12).

This sinful nature is deceptive. Jeremiah said in Jeremiah 17:9 that, "The heart is deceitful above all things, and desperately wicked: who can know it?" God alone knows how wicked the carnal heart of man is. We don't know our own hearts. We need the Holy Spirit to search our hearts. Someone said, "We need the Holy Spirit to give us a guided tour of our own individual hearts."

How does the carnal mind manifest itself? It causes us to rebel against God and say, "No, I'll take my own way." The carnal mind retards spiritual growth in the lives of believers. This was the problem at Corinth. Paul said in I Corinthians 3:1 that, "I, brethren, could not speak unto you as unto spiritual

(Spirit filled Christians and growing), but as unto carnal, even as unto babes in Christ."

The carnal mind causes instability and compromise as in the life of Peter before Pentecost. The carnal mind causes division as was modeled at Corinth. The carnal mind hinders usefulness as in the case of the disciples. The carnal mind often nullifies our witness. It causes pride, jealousy, bitterness and self centeredness. It makes one easy prey to Satan in times of temptation. Dr. B.F. Neely said, "Carnality is that which rises up and tries to open the door every time the devil knocks from without. We can have clean lives only when we get at the troublemaker and through Divine grace get rid of the traitorous doorkeeper."

What is the remedy for the carnal mind? Some say the remedy is growth. The Bible teaches growth in grace but not growth into grace. You cannot grow the carnal mind out of your heart any more than you can grow the weeds out of your garden. Some say the remedy for the carnal mind is suppression. They claim you can never be free from the carnal mind. They say the only thing you can do is suppress it and hope it does not embarrass you at an unguarded moment. Others say that death is the answer. There have been those that believe you get dying grace just before the event of death. One man and his wife believed that way. The wife was very ill and felt she was dying. She called for the pastor and other praying people to come and pray for her to get dying grace. As they prayed the presence of the Lord filled the room. She felt she had received dying grace. But, God healed her, and she did not die. There was a new victory in her life. Her husband saw the difference and said, "I want what she has." They discovered that God had sanctified her wholly. They were both instrumental in starting a school to prepare preachers to proclaim the message of scriptural holiness.

The Word of God says that crucifixion and cleansing is the remedy for the carnal mind. The Apostle Paul says in Romans 6:6, "Knowing this, that our old man (the carnal mind) is crucified (put to death) with Him, that the body of sin (the carnal mind) might be destroyed (not suppressed), that henceforth we should not serve sin (that we should not be slaves to the carnal mind)." Crucifixion speaks of cleansing, purging and the death of the carnal mind.

How can you experience this cleansing? First of all, one must get genuinely converted. The new birth is holiness begun. Next, we must recognize the need of heart cleansing. The Bible reveals the need, and human experience confirms it.

Dr. E. R. Overly was a holiness preacher from Carlisle, Kentucky, in Nicholas County. I heard him preach at the Mt. Carmel Camp Meeting and worked with him in the Hancock County Camp Meeting in Findlay, Ohio. I heard him testify as to how he got saved. After he was converted, he sat in the "amen corner" of the Methodist Church. He would amen the preacher. He often testified and led in public prayer. One day someone did something or said something he did not like. He said that something slid down his arm and caused his fist to double up, and he wanted to fight. He knew that a Christian ought not do that. He went to the locust thicket and had a prayer meeting and asked the Lord to forgive him. Peace was restored to his heart along with assurance that he was right with God. He went back to the amen corner and "amened" the preacher, testified and prayed in church. Things went well for a period of time. Then someone else did something that made him angry. There was the same reaction as before. Knowing a Christian should not fight, again he went to the locust thicket and had another prayer meeting. He went on to say how unfortunate it would have been if he would have had to keep running to the locust thicket all his life. He found that God had something more for him. He found the remedy for that something inside that wanted to fight and strike back when mistreated. He saw the need of a clean heart got entirely sanctified and preached it for many years until God called him home.

John says in I John 1:7, "If we walk in the light, as He is in the light, we have fellowship one with another, and the blood of Jesus Christ His Son cleanseth us from all sin." The sinner walks in darkness. The believer walks in light. As we walk in the light we enjoy wonderful fellowship with God and His people. As we continue to walk in the light the Holy Spirit will lead us into the experience of inner cleansing from the carnal mind. The blood of Christ is the agent of cleansing. That cleansing is both instantaneous and continuous, as we continue to walk in the light.

There is a remedy for the carnal mind. All clash and conflict between our will and God's will can be removed.

Ann was a six year old girl. She learned to sing in DVBS:

> If I had a scooter new
> I would sometime share with you.
> If I had an apple bright,
> I would let you have a bite.

Ann had no scooter, and extra apples could be had easily. These things presented no problem to her. She did have a bicycle that she loved very much. Her daddy said "Let's sing like this."

> If I had a bike so new,
> I would sometime share with you.

Ann's face clouded up. Her lips trembled. Tears welled up, and she sobbed, "No, daddy, I don't want to sing it that way."

God wants to cleanse from our hearts that selfish, self centered disposition, called the carnal mind, that wants its own way.

First, we must be born of the Spirit. We must then recognize the need of this inner cleansing. As we then walk in the light, confess the need, and surrender completely to God's will, we must by faith experience the blood that cleanseth from all sin.

Two Prayers of Jesus

"Then said Jesus, Father forgive them; for they know not what they do" (Luke 23:34).

"Sanctify them through Thy truth: Thy word is truth" (John 17:17).

These two verses of scripture contain two prayers or parts of two prayers of our Lord and Savior, Jesus Christ. One prayer was prayed from the cross, and the other was prayed on Thursday evening just prior to going to the cross. We wish to examine these two prayers in the light of three very simple questions. For whom did Christ pray? For what did Christ pray? Why did Christ pray as He did on each occasion?

The first prayer we wish to look at is the one in Luke 23:34 where Jesus said, "Father forgive them; for they know not what they do." This prayer was the first of seven times that Jesus spoke while hanging on the cross.

Whom was Christ praying for in this prayer? We need not look far to discover those for whom He was praying. Judas, the one that betrayed Him, may very well have been in the shadows nearby. I believe He included Judas in that prayer. Those that accused Him falsely, those that mocked Him and condemned Him unjustly were without a doubt in the midst. Soldiers that scourged Him, crowned Him with thorns and drove nails into His hands and feet looked on. Those that spit upon Him, cursed Him, reviled Him and struck Him with sticks and the palms of their hands stood by watching Him die. In that crowd were those that were indifferent, those that refused to believe on Him and those that openly rejected Him as the Son of God, the Savior of the world. Jesus was praying for His enemies. He was praying for sinful humanity. I believe that prayer reaches out to every sinner that has ever lived and ever will live.

There is no greater sin than to reject Jesus Christ the one that died on the cross of Calvary for your redemption. A person may be moral, attend church regularly, be respected in the community and be a Christ rejecter at the same time.

Jesus was praying for sinners when He said, "Father, forgive them; for they know not what they do."

We ask our second question. What did Christ pray for in this prayer? The answer is very obvious. He was praying that sinners might be forgiven or pardoned from their sin. When one is pardoned he is released from the penalty and justice he rightly deserves. The Bible makes it clear that as sinners we deserved death. In Ezekiel 18:20 the prophet said, "The soul that sinneth, it shall die." In Romans 6:23 the Apostle Paul said, "The wages of sin is death." The death penalty hangs over the head of every sinner. Christ died for every sinner. He became our substitute. He paid our penalty. The Apostle Peter tells us in I Peter 2:24 that Christ "His own self bare our sins in His own body on the tree."

If Christ purchased and provided a pardon for every sinner why are not all sinners pardoned? I heard or read this story about three boys that grew up together in a county seat town in Kentucky. We will call them Tom, Bob and Sam. These boys went to school together, played together and got in mischief together. They had many happy times together as boys. In time their ways parted. Bob went to the university and graduated. He went to law school and passed his bar exam. He eventually got into politics and scaled the political ladder and became governor of the Commonwealth of Kentucky. Tom settled down in his home area. He was a hard-working family man. He was known to be an honest law-abiding citizen. He was well respected in his community. Sam committed a crime and was sentenced to the penitentiary. After some years Tom and Bob were together once again. They reminisced over the good times they shared as boys. Their conversation turned to Sam, the third member of their party. Tom reminded Bob that Sam was in prison. He further reminded Bob that as governor he had it in his power to grant Sam a pardon. Bob took this under consideration, and in time the pardon was granted. It was sealed with the seal of the Commonwealth of Kentucky. It bore the signature of the governor. It was official. The pardon was entrusted to Tom for delivery to Sam. The day came when Tom went to see Sam in prison. They reminisced and talked of their happy times together as boys. Tom reminded Sam that their mutual friend, Bob, was now governor of the Commonwealth of Kentucky. He reminded him that Bob had it in his power to grant him a pardon. He asked Sam what he would do if in fact he were given a pardon. Sam's eyes filled with hate, and he said, "I would go back to the county seat town and murder the judge that sentenced me to this penitentiary." Tom said, "Sam, I have in my pocket a pardon. Your name is on it. It is signed by the governor and sealed with the seal of the Commonwealth of Kentucky. It is official. I'm your friend and would love to see you freed from this penitentiary. I would love to see you have another chance to go home and live as a law-abiding citizen. While I'm your friend I am also a friend of the Commonwealth of Kentucky. Since you are not willing to go home and live as a law-abiding citizen, I cannot give you this pardon." Tom tore up the pardon and threw it in the trash. If Sam would have met one condition, he could have been pardoned. The condition was to be willing to live as a law-abiding citizen.

Pardon has been provided for every sinner. The only reason many people have not been pardoned is that they have not met the conditions. They have not repented of their sins and put their faith in Jesus Christ for the forgiveness of their sins.

Jesus prayed that sinners might be forgiven. Peter tells us in II Peter 3:9 that God is "not willing that any should perish (or be eternally lost), but that all should come to repentance."

But why did Christ pray as He did in this prayer? This is not the way many and most would act when mistreated and abused as Jesus had been. Many would be seeking to get even. They would be seeking to get revenge, to strike back and settle the score. I think the chief reason Christ prayed as He did was LOVE. Paul writes in Romans 5:7,8 and says, "For scarcely for a righteous man will one die: yet peradventure for a good man some would even dare to die. But God commendeth His love toward us, in that, while we were yet sinners, Christ died for us."

Jesus said, regarding these sinners for whom He prayed, "They know not what they do." Sin has a maddening effect. Jesus told us about the prodigal son and said that when he was in the hog pen "He came to himself." He had not been thinking right, reasoning right or acting rationally. Sinners are often so blinded by sin that they harm their own bodies, mistreat their companion, abuse their children, endanger society and sin against Christ, their only hope of salvation and heaven. How unreasonable it is!

"For God so loved the world (all mankind), that He gave His only begotten Son, that whosoever believeth in Him should not perish, but have everlasting life" (John 3:16). Christ loves sinners and wants none to perish, be lost, be damned or to go to hell. He wants all to be saved. That is why he died, and that is why He prayed this prayer.

The second prayer we're considering is in John 17:17 where Jesus prayed, "Sanctify them through Thy truth: Thy word is truth."

This prayer was prayed by Christ on Thursday evening prior to the crucifixion. The last supper was now history. Judas had gone out to betray his Lord. Christ was about to go to the garden of Gethsemane. Jesus now prayed what is known as His High Priestly Prayer contained in John 17. The great climax of that prayer is in verse seventeen where He says, "Sanctify them through Thy truth: Thy word is truth."

For whom did Christ pray in this prayer? There are three petitions in this prayer. The first petition is in verses 1-5 where He prays for Himself. In verse five He prays, "And now, O Father, glorify Thou me with Thine own self with the glory which I had with Thee before the world was." When Jesus came into the world as a baby in Bethlehem, He temporarily laid aside the glory that was rightfully His. He is now ready to return to the Father and prays that the glory temporarily laid aside might now be restored.

In verses 6-19 He prays for His immediate disciples. In verse six He said, "I have manifested Thy name unto the men which Thou gavest me out of the world: Thine they were, and Thou gavest them me, and they have KEPT THY WORD." Jesus said His disciples had been saved out of the world and were obedient to the word. In verse eight Jesus said, "They have believed that Thou didst send me." Jesus said that they were believers in Him as sent from the Father. In verse nine He said, "I pray not for the world, but for them which Thou hast given me; for they are Thine." In this verse Jesus makes it clear that He is not praying for the world, the unregenerated or the sinner. In verse ten He said, "I am glorified in them." Certainly, Christ is glorified in those that love Him, obey Him, trust Him and serve Him. He is not glorified in those that blaspheme His name and sin in word, thought and deed every day.

Jesus said in verse twelve that "None of them is lost but the son of perdition that the scripture might be fulfilled." Jesus once again makes it clear that He is praying for Christians, not sinners. He refers to Judas. In Acts 1:25 Luke tells us that "Judas by transgression fell." He was not predestined to be lost as some might want us to believe. He was lost as a result of his own wilful choice and action. John 17:14 states, "The world hateth them." This is further evidence that they were regenerated. The Apostle Paul stated in II Timothy 3:12 that "All that will live Godly in Christ Jesus shall suffer persecution."

Jesus not only prayed for His disciples, but He also prayed for all future believers in John 17:20 where He said, "Neither pray I for these alone, but for them also which shall believe on me through their word." This includes every believer, every born again Christian, that has ever lived and that will ever live.

In the first prayer in Luke 23:34 Jesus prayed for sinners. In this prayer in John 17 He is praying for born again believers.

Now we consider what Christ prayed for when He said, "Sanctify them through Thy truth; Thy word is truth." The answer to the question is very obvious. He prayed for His disciples and all believers to be sanctified. The word sanctify is derived from two Latin words. One word is sanctus, an adjective, meaning holy. The other word is facere, a verb, meaning to make. It literally means to make holy. The sentence is imperative. The subject is understood. Jesus is addressing the Father. He is literally praying "Father, make my disciples holy." The dictionary tells us the word sanctify means two things. It means to set apart, to dedicate, to separate and to consecrate. It also means to purify, to cleanse and to make holy. In verse nineteen Jesus said, "For their sakes I sanctify myself, that they also might be sanctified through the truth." He is not saying for their sakes I make myself holy. He was holy from all eternity. In Hebrews 4:15 we read He "was in all points tempted as we are, yet without sin." Jesus was saying, for their sakes I set myself apart, or I dedicate myself, to go to the cross and die in order that my disciples and all believers might be made holy.

In Luke 23:34 Jesus prayed for sinners to be forgiven. In John 17:17 Jesus prayed for believers to be sanctified.

Why did Jesus pray this prayer? Jesus was depending on His disciples to carry on His work in the world. He was counting on them to preach the gospel to all the world and to build His church. He recognized that they were inadequate for the task. He said you need to "Wait for the promise of the Father." He said, "You need to be endued with power from on high."

This deeper need was very evident in the lives of the disciples. Look at James and John. They were greedy and self-seeking. In Matthew 20:21 we have the record of where their mother came to Jesus and said, "Grant that these my two sons may sit, the one on Thy right hand and the other on the left, in Thy kingdom." Mark said in Mark 10 :37 that James and John made this request. It may be that they put their mother up to requesting for them. The request reveals greed and self seeking. James and John also manifested an evil temper. Jesus was on His way to Jerusalem and passed through Samaria. The Samaritans did not receive Jesus the way James and John thought He should be received. They said in Luke 9:54-56, "Wilt Thou that we command fire to come down from heaven and consume them?" Jesus rebuked them saying, "Ye know not what manner of spirit ye are of, for the Son of man did not come to destroy men's lives, but to save them." Jesus was saying, "Father, I want to use James and John. I recognize so many good things about them. However, I can't use them with this greedy and self centered spirit. I can't use them with this old explosive disposition. If they don't get their way they want to let people have it. Father, I want you to sanctify James and John."

Then there was Peter, a double-minded man. James said in James 1:8 that "A double-minded man is unstable in all his ways." Peter made two great confessions. The first is recorded in Matthew 16:13-16 which says, "When Jesus came into the coasts of Caesarea Philippi, He asked His disciples, saying, Whom do men say that I the Son of man am? And they said, Some say that Thou art John the Baptist: some Elias; and others, Jeremias, or one of the prophets. He saith unto them, But whom say ye that I am? And Simon Peter answered and said, Thou art the Christ, the Son of the Living God." Jesus immediately replied in Matthew 16:17 and said, "Blessed art thou Simon Barjona: for flesh and blood hath not revealed this unto thee, but my Father which is in heaven." This was truly a great confession. Then on another occasion many who had followed Jesus had turned away, and Jesus spoke to the twelve as recorded in John 6:67-69 and said, "Will ye also go away? Then Simon Peter answered Him, Lord, to whom shall we go? Thou hast the words of eternal life, and we believe and are sure that Thou art that Christ, the Son of the living God." This was truly a second great confession by Peter. But Peter was slow to comprehend the meaning of the cross at Caesarea Philippi as recorded in Matthew 16:20-23 where Jesus "Then charged He His disciples that they should tell no man that He was Jesus the Christ. From that time forth began Jesus to shew unto His disciples, how that He must go unto Jerusalem, and suffer many things of the elders and chief priests and scribes, and be killed, and be raised again the third day. Then Peter took Him, and began to rebuke Him, saying, Be it far from Thee, Lord: this shall not be unto Thee. But He turned, and said unto Peter, get thee behind me, Satan: thou art an offence unto me: for thou savourest not the things that be of God, but those that be of men."

On Thursday, the day before the crucifixion, the disciples were in the upper room with Jesus. In Matthew 26:30-35 we read, "And when they had sung a hymn, they went out into the Mount of Olives. Then saith Jesus unto them, All ye shall be offended because of me this night: for it is written, I will smite the shepherd, and the sheep of the flock shall be scattered abroad. But after I am risen again, I will go before you into Galilee. Peter answered and said unto Him, Though all men shall be offended because of Thee, yet will I never be offended. Jesus said unto him, Verily I say unto thee, that this night before the cock crow, thou shalt deny me thrice. Peter said unto Him, Though I should die with Thee, yet will I not deny Thee. Likewise also said all the disciples."

It was the next day, on Friday, that Jesus was arrested in the Garden of Gethsemane. Jesus was led away to the high priest. Matthew 26:58 tells us that "Peter followed Him afar off." In Mark 14:67-72 Mark says, "And when she (the maid) saw Peter warming himself, she looked upon him, and said, And thou also wast with Jesus of Nazareth. But he denied, saying, I know not, neither understand I what thou sayest. And he went out into the porch, and the cock crew. And a maid saw him again, and began to say to them that stood by, this is one of them. And he denied it again. And a little after, they that stood by said again to Peter, Surely thou art one of them, for thou art a Galilean, and thy speech agreeth thereto. But he began to curse and to say, I know not this man of whom ye speak. And the second time the cock crew. And Peter called to mind the word that Jesus said unto him, Before the cock crows twice, thou shalt deny me thrice. And when he thought thereon, he wept."

When Jesus prayed, "Sanctify them" He was praying for Peter. Jesus saw great potential in Peter, but Peter was double minded. He boasted that he would never fail Christ, but in a matter of hours he cursed and denied that he ever knew Christ. Peter failed, but he wept and repented for his failure. I believe Jesus was saying, "Father, I can't use Peter like this. I want you to sanctify him. I want you to cleanse his heart from that compromising carnal spirit within and empower him with the Holy Spirit."

Jesus prayed for Thomas. Thomas was full of doubts. Jesus prayed that he might be sanctified and full of faith.

All the disciples were weak, self seeking and unstable. The night before the crucifixion they were arguing as to which one was the greatest. The record is in Luke 22:24 where the scripture says, "There was also a strife among them, which of them should be accounted the greatest." Jesus wanted to use these men but could not use them like this. He prayed that they might be cleansed from carnal weakness, selfseeking and compromise. He prayed that they might be sanctified.

He prayed for them to be sanctified that "They might be kept from the evil" (John 17:15), "That they may be one" (John 17:22) with God and each other, "That they might have His joy fulfilled in them" (John 17:13), "That the world may know that Thou hast sent me" (John 17:23), "That the love wherewith Thou hast loved me may be in them" (John 17:26), and "I in them" (John 17:26).

Christ prayed for sinners in Luke 23:34 saying, "Father, forgive them; for they know not what they do." He was praying for sinners to be forgiven that none should be lost. He loves sinners and wants all to be saved.

Christ prayed for believers in John 17:17 when He prayed, "Sanctify them through Thy truth: Thy word is truth." He prayed for believers to get sanctified that they might be cleansed from the greedy, self-centered sinful nature. He prayed they might be sanctified in order that they might be cleansed from the carnal mind that would tend to draw them away from Christ and back into sin and spiritual failure. He prayed for them to be sanctified because He wanted to use them to take the gospel to all the world, and they needed cleansing and the empowering of the Holy Spirit to be equipped for the task.

Where is Jesus today? He is at the right hand of the Father. What is He doing? He is interceding for us. That means He is praying for us. For what is He praying? He is still praying for sinners to be saved and believers to be sanctified. You are on His prayer list. He is counting on us to be His witnesses in the world. To be equipped for the task we must be pure, holy and sanctified vessels filled and empowered by the Holy Spirit.

Entire Consecration

Romans 6:12-22

"Yield yourselves unto God, as those that are alive from the dead, and your members as instruments of righteousness unto God. Even so now yield your members servants to righteousness unto holiness" (Romans 6:13b,19b).

The Apostle Paul personifies sin as a cruel ruler and slave master. Paul states that we are either slaves of sin or slaves of righteousness, depending on to whom and to what we yield ourselves.

Paul addresses these Roman Christians as "those who were slaves of sin." Here he uses the past tense. He speaks of what they used to be. Now, he speaks of them as "being alive from the dead." Then he says, "being made free from sin ye became the servants of righteousness." They had experienced a radical transformation. They had been freed from sin's slavery and slave master and were now slaves of righteousness. Thus, Paul makes it clear that he is addressing Christians, those alive in Christ and freed from the slavery of sin. They had passed from spiritual death to spiritual life.

Paul appeals to these born-again believers to yield themselves to God and to yield their members as instruments unto God to be "servants to righteousness unto holiness."

Formerly their members were yielded to sinful practices, but they have been freed from that way of living. Now Paul says for them to be just as zealous in yielding their members in the service of righteousness and holiness as they formerly were in yielding their members in the practice of sin and unrighteousness.

Consecration differs from repentance. Repentance relates to sin and punishment. Consecration relates to the will and service of God. Repentance involves the renunciation of all our sins. Consecration is the yielding of all our plans, possessions, life and future to the perfect will of God. Repentance is giving up the bad. Consecration is giving up the good. The motive of repentance is to escape the wrath of God. The motive of consecration is love for Jesus. We want to be like Him. We want to please Him and serve Him.

The Bible calls sinners to repentance. "God commandeth all men everywhere to repent" (Acts 17:30). The Bible calls believers to consecrate. "I beseech you therefore, brethren, (Christians), by the mercies of God, that ye present (yield) your bodies a living sacrifice, holy, acceptable unto God, which is your reasonable service. And be not conformed to this world: but be ye transformed by the renewing of your mind, that ye may prove what is that good, and acceptable, and perfect, will of God" (Romans 12:1,2).

Entire consecration is a step beyond repentance. It involves such a detailed yielding to God and dying out of self that no sinner, lukewarm church member or backslider can possibly do it. It can only be done by a born-again Christian in an up to date relationship with Jesus Christ. A spirit of gratitude wells up in the heart of one freed from the slavery of sin.

Stories have been told of slave days here in the United States. Stories of slaves on the auction block. Hard cruel slave masters would be prepared to bid. A kind gentleman would step forward and purchase the slave. He would then give the slave his or her freedom. The slave would be overcome with emotion. The once slave, now free, would, with tears, fall at the feet of the man who set him or her free. Expressions of love, appreciation and gratitude would follow along with a desire to serve the new master forever.

Such a spirit of gratitude wells up in the heart of a new convert who has just been freed from the slavery of sin. There is love for Jesus. There is a desire to be all His and to serve Him with our all.

Consecration also differs from sanctification. Consecration is man's work of yielding to God. Sanctification is God's work of purifying the heart. God cannot consecrate for you, and you cannot purify your own heart. You must consecrate. God must sanctify.

This difference became an issue in 1946 when the (RSV) Revised Standard Version of the New Testament was published. One member of the revision committee said there was no difference between the terms consecration and sanctification. But the Webster's Dictionary does make a difference. The definition of consecrate and sanctify is the same to a point. Both are defined to "make sacred or to set apart to a sacred purpose." The temple, the temple furnishings, the priests and the sacrificial animals were all consecrated or sanctified in that sense.

The definition of consecration terminates at that point while the definition of sanctify goes further. It means "to make free from sin, to cleanse from moral corruption and pollution, and to purify."

For this reason a number of scholars requested the revision committee of the (RSV) Revised Standard Version to change the word "consecrate" to "sanctify" in eighteen specific passages. The committee complied in full in the 1952 edition.

Consecration comes after repentance and regeneration and precedes heart cleansing in entire sanctification. Repentance precedes the new birth. Consecration precedes entire sanctification.

All born-again believers are in a measure consecrated to God. The disciples left all to follow Jesus. They were in a sense consecrated but were not entirely consecrated. Some believers yield more quickly than others. Some things are easier to yield than others. A friend of mine began consecrating to God by yielding his car. He said, "That was really not difficult. It was ready for the junk pile anyway." There are usually one or two points that are more difficult and last to yield. The Rich Young Ruler came running to Jesus and asked, "What good thing shall I do, that I may have eternal life?" Jesus named six commandments which deal with man's relationship with man. He said, "All these things have I kept from my youth up: what lack I yet?" Jesus said, "Go sell that thou hast, and give to the poor, and thou shalt have treasure in heaven: and come and follow me." The young man "went away sorrowful" (Matthew 19:16-22). His possessions were the one thing that stood in his way of surrendering or consecrating all.

Jesus wants total yieldedness of plans, ambitions, possessions, future, and our all. All born-again believers are called upon to consecrate entirely. Paul says in verse thirteen, "yield yourselves unto God." When you yield yourself you yield your all.

J. B. Chapman told of an Indian who related his consecration. He said, "I brought my pony and put it on the altar, but no blessing came. I added my blanket and my tepee, but no blessing came. I added my squaw and my papoose, but no blessing came. But when I cried and this poor Indian, too, O Lord, the blessing came."

When we yield ourselves, all our members are included. Francis R. Havergal wrote, "Take my life, and let it be consecrated Lord to Thee. Take my HANDS, and let them move at the impulse of Thy love. Take my FEET, and let them be swift and beautiful for Thee. Take my VOICE, and let me sing, always, only for my King. Take my LIPS, and let them be filled with messages from Thee. Take my SILVER and my GOLD, not a mite would I withhold. Take my WILL and make it Thine; it shall be no longer mine. Take my HEART; it is Thine own. It shall be Thy royal throne. Take my LOVE, my God, I pour at Thy feet its treasure store. Take MYSELF, and I will be ever, only, all for Thee."

Consecration is not to a denomination or an organization. It is not to God's service. Consecration is to God. Consecration is the willingness, the resolution and the purpose to be, to go, to do and if need be to suffer all God's will for me. To consent to these willingly, without reservation is complete, perfect and entire consecration. Sanctification is conditioned upon such a consecration and faith in the blood of Jesus Christ.

A defective, incomplete or half-hearted consecration blocks the way to sanctification. G. D. Watson said "Unless consecration reaches the place of entirety the soul will slip back and be consecrating itself over and over again a thousand times without gaining a distinct step of victory or making any positive progress." Consecration must be entire. "So likewise whosoever he be of you that forsaketh not ALL that he hath, he cannot be my disciple." All means all!

The word YIELD is in the aorist tense of the Greek language. It denotes a decisive, definite, dedication made once for all to God. I was married on August 30, 1958. It was 'til death do us part. I have never had to be remarried. My marriage is still in effect. On March 9, 1952, I gave God my all, and I've never changed my mind. It is still in effect.

Entire consecration is yielding all to God for all time and eternity. When Alfred Cookman of early Methodism consecrated himself to God he said, "I am wholly (entirely) and forever (eternally) Thine."

Consecration includes the known and the unknown. As the contents of the unknown future are revealed, we keep our consecration current by continually saying yes to God's will.

When perfectly yielded to God without reservation for all time and eternity one can drive a stake and reach a place of anchorage with God and sing "Tis done, the great transaction's done. I am my Lord's and He is mine ... Now rest my long divided heart; fixed on this blissful center rest, nor ever from my Lord depart; to Him who merits all my love."

Consecration brings me to the place of maximum openness and yieldedness to the will of God. I am totally God's. He can do with me as He chooses. There is no resistance to His will. I am His temple for Him to indwell. I am His instrument for Him to use. I am His channel for Him to flow through. I am His clay for Him to mold into His likeness. I am His property for Him to superintend, manage, care and provide for. He is sovereign and Lord of all.

Consecration prepares the way for cleansing. No one is converted until he repents of sin. No one is entirely sanctified until he or she has consecrated everything to God.

In 1983 I had kidney surgery. The doctor was not sure if the kidney was cancerous or not. He said, "We won't know for certain until we operate." He went on to say, "If we find that it is cancerous, we will take the kidney." I'm very grateful the kidney was not cancerous. But, I had to submit. I had to surrender. I had to yield to the hand of the surgeon. Even so we must submit, surrender and yield to God before we can be sanctified.

Consecration paves the way for self crucifixion. Just as Gethsemane preceded Golgotha, consecration precedes crucifixion. Jesus gave Himself to die, and so must I give myself in total submission, consecration and surrender to experience the crucifixion to the carnal self. Paul said in Galations 2:20, "I am crucified with Christ: nevertheless I live; yet not I, but Christ liveth in me: and the life which I now live in the flesh I live by the faith of the Son of God, who loved me, and gave Himself for me."

According to Romans 6:22 consecration enables one to have "fruit unto holiness, and the end everlasting life." When entirely consecrated to God there springs within the heart a consciousness that I am all God's. I remember when I came to the end of myself at the altar of consecration. I knew of nothing that was not surrendered. I said to the Lord, "If there is anything else, show me, and I'll surrender that as well."

When the gift is complete, entire, eternally and forever God's you have the right to claim the promise that "the altar sanctifies the gift" (Matthew23:19) for "faithful is He that calleth you, who also will do it" (I Thessalonians 5:24).

A. M. Hill in his book Holiness in The Book of Romans, quotes Isaiah Reid in his prayer of consecration for holiness. "O Lord, in view of this thing Thou hast besought me to do, I hereby do now really consecrate myself unreservedly to Thee, for all time and eternity. My time, my talents, my hands, my feet, lips, will, my all. My property, my reputation, my entire being, a living sacrifice to be and to do all Thy will pertaining to me. Especially at this time do I, Thy regenerate child, put my case into Thy hands for the cleansing of my nature from indwelling sin. I seek the sanctification of my soul."

He adds this pledge of faith. "Now, as I have given myself away, I will, from this time forth, regard myself as Thine. I believe Thou dost accept the offering I bring. I put all on the altar. I believe the altar sanctifieth the gift. I believe the blood is applied now, as I comply with the terms of Thy salvation. I believe that Thou dost now cleanse me from all sin."

Any believer who thus consecrates entirely and eternally to God has a right to believe the promises of God that He does then and there keep His Word and cleanse the heart from all sin. It would dishonor God not to believe it. But, it would be presumptuous to try to believe if the consecration is incomplete.

God is looking for people who will totally consecrate themselves to Him that He might cleanse and empower them with His Holy Spirit and use them in His kingdom for His glory.

The Need of The Thessalonian Church

I Thessalonians 1; and 3:7-13
"For this is the will of God, even your sanctification, that ye should abstain from fornication" (I Thessalonians 4:3).

Thessalonica was one of the leading cities of Macedonia in the time of the Apostle Paul. He first visited Thessalonica on his second missionary journey. He was not there long until he was driven out of town by certain wicked men that were opposed to his teaching and preaching. He went west about fifty miles to Berea. Those same men that chased him from Thessalonica followed him and managed also to chase him from Berea. He went south to Athens. Paul sent his young traveling companion, Timothy, back to Thessalonica to instruct and establish this infant church and its people. Timothy later returned and joined Paul. By this time Paul was at Corinth.

Timothy reported that the Christians of Thessalonica were courageously enduring much persecution. In the meantime, since Paul had been there, some of their number had died. Some died of natural causes and others possibly due to persecution. Some of their living loved ones were concerned that the deceased might miss out on some of the benefits of Christ's second coming. In each of the five chapters of this epistle Paul mentions the second coming of Jesus. In chapter four, verses thirteen through eighteen, Paul makes it clear that the deceased will rise first when Christ returns, and those living and ready will join them in the air, and "so shall they ever be with the Lord. Wherefore comfort one another with these words." Paul assures these believers that the deceased in Christ will not miss out on any of the benefits of Christ's second coming.

There are three things we want to notice about these believers at Thessalonica. First, they were converts of the Apostle Paul's ministry. Second, they were a great comfort to

Paul. Third, they were still a concern to Paul.

The seventeenth chapter of Acts gives us the record of Paul's ministry at Thessalonica on his second missionary journey. The fourth verse says, "And some of them believed, and consorted with Paul and Silas; and of the devout Greeks a great multitude, and of the chief women not a few." All of the Jews did not get angry at Paul and drive him from Thessalonica. Some repented and believed on Christ as their personal Savior. These new converts joined up with Paul and Silas in their ministry. A great multitude of Greeks or Gentiles were converted. The number was so large that they did not try to count them. They simply said it was a great multitude. Furthermore, a large delegation of the leading ladies of the city repented and trusted Christ as their Savior. It may have included the mayor's wife and the wives of the city council or whatever the equivalent was in that day. This was a great revival. In the sixth verse of this chapter Paul was accused of "turning the world upside down." We know they were wrong in their accusation. When revival comes things are turned right side up. Wrongs are made right. Broken relationships are repaired. Lives are changed, and homes are saved from destruction.

There is much evidence in First Thessalonians, chapter one, that these people were genuinely converted.

In verse one, Paul says, they were "in God the Father and in the Lord Jesus Christ." That little preposition IN tells us much about these people. There is all the difference in the world in being IN Christ and being OUTSIDE of Christ. They were IN harmony with Christ. They were IN fellowship with Christ, and they were IN love with Christ.

In verse two, Paul says, "We give thanks to God always for you all, making mention of you in our prayers." Paul, without doubt, had a great prayer list. As he came down his list and began praying for the believers at Thessalonica, he had to stop and praise God. He rejoiced in what God did in the revival at Thessalonica on his second missionary journey. Many lives were transformed. and for this Paul gave God glory and praise.

In verse three, Paul said, "Remembering without ceasing your work of faith, and labor of love, and patience of hope in our Lord Jesus Christ." They had a faith that worked, a love that labored, and a hope that endured.

In verse six, he said, "Ye became followers of us, and of the Lord, having received the Word in much affliction with joy of the Holy Ghost." Paul remembers that in that great revival these folk were marvelously delivered from their old heathen ways and gloriously saved. He said you followed us as we followed Christ, or you imitated us as we imitated our Lord. They suffered great persecution as a result of their Christian testimony. It was costly to be a Christian. They could lose their job, be disowned by their family, go to jail or be put to death. They did not feel sorry for themselves and complain about their situation. They were rejoicing in the privilege of suffering for Jesus sake.

In verse seven, Paul said, "Ye were ensamples to all that believe in Macedonia and Achaia." They were examples and models of what a true Christian ought to be, how he ought to live and act. If someone wanted to know what a Christian was like, Paul pointed to these Thessalonian Christians. They were good models of Bible Christianity.

In verse eight, Paul said, "In every place your faith to Godward is spread abroad." They were good witnesses, and the news of their conversion was being talked about all over Macedonia and Greece. Paul did not need to tell anyone about these converts. The news was already out. When people get genuinely converted, the word travels fast.

In verse nine, the apostle said, "Ye turned to God from idols to serve the living and true God." Here is evidence of true repentance. They turned from their old idolatrous ways to serve the one true God. They turned one hundred eighty degrees. They turned from sin to the Savior.

In verse ten, Paul said, "They were waiting for His Son from heaven." They were waiting and expecting Jesus to return.

There is every evidence that these people to whom Paul was writing were not sinners. They were not lukewarm Christians. They were not backsliders. They were born-again believers in an up to date relationship with their Lord and Savior, Jesus

Christ. They were converted under the ministry of the Apostle Paul.

In chapter three, verses seven through nine, we discover that these believers were a great comfort to the Apostle Paul. Timothy had just returned from Thessalonica and brought with him a good report that brought comfort to the heart of the apostle. Paul had been going through some tough times. In verse seven, he mentions "afflictions and distress." He had been driven out of Thessalonica and Berea with a threat on his life. Their intention, without doubt, was not just to drive him from town. Their apparent intention was to kill him. But God was not through with the apostle, and his life was spared.

Paul went from Berea to Athens. This was the intellectual center. The philosophers and great thinkers had little time for the religion that Paul preached involving Jesus Christ who died on a cross for the sins of the world. There were few converts at Athens and no record of a church that was planted.

Paul went from Athens to Corinth. He found it was a difficult place, and there was much opposition. In verse five of chapter eighteen of Acts we read that "Paul was pressed in the spirit." He may have been under great pressure. He could well have been discouraged, and Satan may have been tempting him to quit his missionary ministry. In the midst of this Timothy arrives with this good report, and Paul is comforted.

The scripture says, "He was comforted by their faith." They had experienced faith for the forgiveness of their sins when Paul was at Thessalonica on his second missionary journey. They had learned to walk by faith and not to depend on their feelings. You have heard about fact, faith and feeling walking on a wall. Feeling tumbled off, and faith tumbled too, but fact remained. Fact brought back faith, and feeling came, too. We all must learn that we cannot depend on feeling. We must have faith anchored in fact. These believers further learned that the Christian life is a fight of faith. We are in spiritual warfare. "For we wrestle not against flesh and blood, but against principalities, against powers, against the rulers of the darkness of this world, against spiritual wickedness in high places. Above all, taking the shield of faith, wherewith ye shall be able to quench all the fiery darts of the wicked" (Ephesians 6:12,16). They also learned, "That the trial of your faith, being much more precious than of gold that perisheth, though it be tried with fire, might be found unto praise and honor and glory at the appearing of Jesus Christ" (I Peter 1:7). Their faith had grown, deepened and increased. If you want your faith to grow, get into the Word of God. "Faith cometh by hearing, and hearing by the Word of God" (Romans 10:17).

Paul was not only comforted by their faith. He was comforted by their standing fast. In spite of suffering and persecution they had not let up spiritually. They had not cooled off in their love for Christ. They remained true to their Lord even if it meant loss of job, rejection of family, jail or death. Paul said in I Thessalonians 3:8, "We live, if ye stand fast in the Lord."

Paul felt it was worth all the beatings, perils, privations, imprisonments and hardships he had experienced to see results like this. I think I can identify with Paul. I have served on the World Gospel Mission Board of Directors for a number of years. I was very discouraged when I went to a board meeting some years ago. A group of missionary candidates appeared before the board to give their testimonies. One of the candidates was a graduate of Mt. Carmel High School and Kentucky Mountain Bible Institute (now College). He had been one of my students. He testified of how he was converted, later sanctified and called to missions while studying at our schools. I was encouraged. I felt that this makes it all worth-while. I was ready to come back and do it all over again.

While these believers were converts of Paul's ministry and a comfort to Paul, they were also a great concern to Paul. That concern is noted in I Thessalonians 3:10-13. Paul was concerned about seeing these believers and discipling them. He was so concerned that he had lost sleep over them.

Paul was concerned about a lack in their faith, according to verse ten. But, chapter one, verse three says they had a "work of faith." They had a faith that worked. In chapter three and verse seven, Paul said, "We were comforted over you in all our affliction and distress by your faith." These folk had experienced saving faith and had grown in that faith. However, they had never experienced sanctifying faith. Paul said, "This is the will of God even your sanctification." Paul was greatly concerned that these believers would get sanctified wholly.

In verse twelve of chapter three we see yet another concern. Paul was concerned that their love would increase. In chapter one, verse three, we read that they had a "labor of love." They had a love for God that caused them to labor for God. When converted, "The love of God is shed abroad in our hearts by the Holy Ghost which is given unto us" (Romans 5:5b). This is the experience of every born-again believer. When entirely sanctified our love is made perfect. "God is love; and he that dwelleth in love dwelleth in God, and God in him. Herein is our love made perfect, that we may have boldness in the day of judgment; because as He is, so are we in this world. There is no fear in love; but perfect love casteth out fear" (I John 4:16-18). How do you get perfect love? You get it by getting entirely sanctified. Paul said to these new converts, "This is the will of God, even your sanctification." The Thessalonian Christians had been saved but had not been sanctified. Sanctification is both a crisis and a process. We must experience the definite crisis. This is followed by a process. Love can increase. Peter spoke of adding charity or love in II Peter 1:7.

Paul was further concerned that these new converts get established. This concern is voiced in I Thessalonians 3:13, "To the end he may stablish your hearts unblameable in holiness."

Carnal weakness is removed when we are sanctified wholly. Peter boasted that he would never fail Christ. Only hours later he cursed and denied that he ever knew Jesus. Peter repented of his failure. He went to Pentecost and experienced heart cleansing and was empowered by the Holy Spirit. It was Peter who stood up on the day of Pentecost and boldly proclaimed the resurrected Christ as the one they had crucified. He got sanctified, and it brought power and stability into his life.

Carnal anger is removed when we are sanctified. I had a good friend in Mt. Carmel Christian High School during my student days. When I first met him he was not a Christian. He had a problem with anger. He got converted. He went on to get sanctified in a second work of grace. He was totally different. God called him to preach, and he has been greatly used of God.

Carnal appetites are removed when we are sanctified. Paul said, "This is the will of God, even your sanctification, THAT YE SHOULD ABSTAIN FROM FORNICATION" (I Thessalonians 4:3). These people had been saved out of heathenism. Fornication, immorality, was a part of their heathen life style. Paul knew if they did not get sanctified that the carnal mind within would tend to pull them back to their old heathen, ungodly, ways.

Paul was further concerned that these converts would be ready for the rapture. He said in I Thessalonians 3:13, "To the end He may stablish your hearts in holiness before God, even our Father, AT THE COMING OF OUR LORD JESUS CHRIST WITH ALL HIS SAINTS." Paul said, "The very God of peace sanctify you wholly; and I pray God your whole spirit and soul and body be preserved blameless UNTO THE COMING OF OUR LORD JESUS CHRIST" (I Thessalonians 5:23).

This group of believers needed to get sanctified in order to get settled spiritually, and so do believers today. This group of believers needed to get sanctified in order to be free from carnal appetites that would tend to pull them back to their former ungodly life style, and so do believers today. This group of believers needed to get sanctified in order to be at their best as witnesses and soul winners, and so do believers today. This group of believers needed to get sanctified to be ready for Christ's return, and so do believers today. "This is the will of God even your sanctification." This is not just for Thessalonian Christians. It is for all Christians. It is God's will. Jesus said, "Not every one that saith unto me, Lord, Lord, shall enter into the kingdom of heaven; but he that doeth the will of my Father which is in heaven" (Matthew 7:21).

Entire Sanctification

I Thessalonians 5:23-24

According to Strong's concordance the words sanctify, sanctified, sanctifieth and sanctification are found 142 times in the Bible.

Webster's Dictionary defines sanctify as: to make sacred or holy, to set apart to a holy or religious use, to consecrate by appropriate rites, to hallow. A second definition is to make free from sin, to cleanse from moral corruption and pollution, to purify. Webster further states that sanctification is the act of God's grace by which the affections of men are purified or alienated from sin and the world, and exalted to supreme love to God.

The Standard Dictionary defines sanctify as: to make holy, render sacred; morally or spiritually pure, cleansed from sin. It defines sanctification as: the gracious work of the Holy Spirit whereby the believer is freed from sin and exalted to holiness of heart.

The words sanctify and sanctification have two basic meanings. One is to set apart or to consecrate. The other is to cleanse, purify, or make holy. These two meanings are clearly noted in John 17:17,19. In verse 17 Jesus prays for His disciples and says, "Sanctify them through Thy truth: Thy word is truth." Here He literally is saying, "Father, make my disciples holy." In verse 19 Jesus says, "For their sakes I sanctify Myself, that they also might be sanctified through the truth." Here He literally is saying, "For their sakes I set myself apart to go to the cross and die in order that they (my disciples) might be made holy."

We sanctify ourselves by consecrating ourselves totally unto God. God sanctifies us by cleansing us from all sin and purifying our hearts. Sanctification is not complete until both have taken place. I must consecrate, and God must cleanse and empower.

In our text we have six fundamental Biblical facts about

entire sanctification.

I. Entire sanctification is a second work of grace.
II. Entire sanctification is an instantaneous work of grace.
III. Entire sanctification is a Divine work of grace.
IV. Entire sanctification is a thorough work of grace.
V. Entire sanctification is a preserving work of grace.
VI. Entire sanctification is an ongoing work of grace.

Entire sanctification is a SECOND work of grace subsequent and following regeneration. The Thessalonian Christians were converted on Paul's second missionary journey. The record is in Acts 17:1-4. Verse four says, "Some of them believed, and consorted with Paul and Silas, and of the devout Greeks a great multitude, and of the chief women not a few." Some Jews believed on Christ as their personal Savior and were converted. A great multitude of Greeks or Gentiles were converted. There was also a large number of the leading women of Thessalonica that were converted in that revival on Paul's second missionary journey.

First Thessalonians chapter one is full of evidence that these people to whom Paul wrote were genuine Christians. In verse one he says, "They were IN God the Father and IN the Lord Jesus Christ". There is all the difference in the world in being IN Christ and being OUTSIDE of Christ. In verse three he says, "Remembering without ceasing your work of faith, and labor of love, and patience of hope in our Lord Jesus Christ." They had a work of faith, labor of love and patience of hope. In verse six Paul says, "Ye became followers of us, and of the Lord, having received the word in much affliction, with joy of the Holy Ghost." The word follower means IMITATOR. Paul said, "They imitated us as we imitated Christ." Persecution was on. It was costly to be a Christian. You might lose your job. Your parents might disown you. You might go to jail or you might die for your faith in Christ. They were facing severe persecution, but they were rejoicing in the privilege of suffering for Jesus sake. In verse seven Paul says, "Ye were ensamples to all that believe in Macedonia and Achaia. They were good examples of Bible Christianity. In verse nine we read, "Ye turned to God from idols to serve the living and true

God." That speaks of true repentance. They had turned from their idolatrous way of living to the one true and living God. They had turned from sin to the Savior. In verse ten it states, "They were waiting for Jesus to return." There is every evidence in chapter one that these people were truly born again and living in an up to date relationship with their Lord and Savior Jesus Christ.

Paul urges these Christians to go on to holiness. In I Thessalonians 4:7 Paul says, "For God hath not called us unto uncleanness, but unto holiness." In I Thessalonians 4:3 he says, "For this is the will of God, even your sanctification, that ye should abstain from fornication." Thus, Paul makes it very clear that entire sanctification is a second work of grace following regeneration.

Second, we note that entire sanctification is an INSTANTANEOUS work of grace. It may be approached gradually, but the moment it is received it comes instantly in a crisis moment.

Look at the disciples at Pentecost. In Acts 2:2,3 we read that "Suddenly there was a rushing mighty wind ... and there appeared cloven tongues like as of fire, and it sat upon each of them." And verse four says, "They were all filled with the Holy Ghost." There was a ten day waiting period that gradually prepared them for that instantaneous crisis moment. Peter testified in the council in Jerusalem recorded in Acts 15:8,9 that their "Hearts were purified by faith, and they were all filled with the Holy Ghost." It happened instantly in a moment in time. Dr. W.B. Godbey translated this text in this way. "The very God of peace sanctify you THIS MOMENT." The word sanctify indicates a complete work done at a point in time. No one ever testified to getting sanctified gradually by growth. We grow in grace, but we do not grow into grace. We must get instantaneously sanctified in a crisis moment and then grow in that grace. Entire sanctification is an instantaneous experience, followed by a life long process of growth into an ever increasing likeness to Christ.

The third thing we note about entire sanctification is that it is a DIVINE work of grace. "The very GOD of peace sanctify you." God is the author of peace and the giver of peace. He is the one that sent the Prince of Peace. May that very GOD SANCTIFY YOU.

God is the originating cause of our sanctification. He planned it in eternity past. In Ephesians 1:4 Paul writes, "According as He (God) hath chosen us in Him (in Christ) before the foundation of the world, that we should be holy and without blame before Him in love."

Jesus is the meritorious cause of our sanctification. The Hebrew writer states in Hebrews 13:12, "Wherefore Jesus also, that He might sanctify the people with His own blood, suffered without the gate." The Apostle Paul wrote in Ephesians 5:25-27, "Christ also loved the church (called out ones or born again ones), and gave Himself for it (the born again): that He might sanctify and cleanse it with the washing of water by the word, that He might present it to Himself a glorious church, not having spot, or wrinkle, or any such thing; but that it should be holy and without blemish."

The Holy Spirit is the efficient cause of our sanctification. In Romans 15:16b Paul says, "being sanctified by the Holy Spirit." In II Thessalonians 2:13b Paul writes, "God hath from the beginning chosen us to salvation through sanctification of the Spirit and belief of the truth."

The Bible is the instrumental cause of our sanctification. In John 17:17 Jesus prayed, "Sanctify them through Thy truth ... " John Wesley interpreted that in this way. "Perfect them in holiness by means of Thy Word."

Faith is the conditional cause of our sanctification. Peter testified in the council in Jerusalem as recorded in Acts 15:8-9 and said, "And God which knoweth the hearts, bare them witness, giving them the Holy Ghost, even as He did unto us (Jews at the Jerusalem); and put no difference between us and them (Jews and Gentiles), purifying their hearts by FAITH." In Acts 26:18b Paul is testifying as to God's revealed purpose for his ministry and says, "That they may receive forgiveness of sins, and inheritance among them which are sanctified by FAITH that is in me (Christ)." Faith will not operate until conditions are met. Repentance precedes faith for justification.

Consecration precedes faith for entire sanctification. Entire sanctification is the work of God Himself in response to man's obedience and faith. "The God of peace (Himself) sanctify you (purify, cleanse and make you holy)." Only God can do this and it happens by FAITH.

Fourth, entire sanctification is a THOROUGH work of grace. "The very God of peace sanctify you wholly (entirely, through and through or make you holy in every part)." God does not want one bit of sin, carnality or self centeredness to remain in the hearts of His children. Paul says, "I pray your whole SPIRIT, SOUL and BODY be preserved blameless unto the coming of our Lord Jesus Christ." Paul is praying for the entire person to be sanctified wholly or entirely. Every part of our being is to be sanctified. Sanctification affects our physical life, emotional life and our spiritual life. It affects our inner-most being and our outer-most conduct.

A sanctified body is a body totally separated from sin and the world and totally separated to God. A sanctified body is a body totally given or surrendered to God Eyes, ears, mind, tongue, hands, feet, time, talents, abilities, resources and future all belong to God. A sanctified body becomes God's dwelling place. Paul writes in I Corinthians 6:19a, "What? Know ye not that your body is the temple of the Holy Ghost which is in you?" He cleanses, fills, empowers and indwells our bodies. He leads, reproves, comforts, encourages, helps, counsels and intercedes for us while we live in these bodies of clay. A sanctified body is used only for the glory of God. In I Corinthians 6:20 we read, "For ye are bought with a price; therefore glorify God in your body and in your spirit which are God's." He employs us in His kingdom to bring Him glory. In spite of our human infirmities He wants to dwell in us, walk in us, beautify us with His presence and use us to bring Him glory. It doesn't matter if we're short or tall, skinny or chubby, handsome or homely, young or old. There is nothing disgraceful about your body. He wants to hallow your body and adorn it with His grace.

Raymond Swauger, along with five other young men from Asbury College, built the first building on the campus of

Mount Carmel High School in the summer of 1925. After graduating from Asbury, he returned to Mount Carmel and spent his life building on the campus of Mount Carmel, Kentucky Mountain Bible Institute, and building churches and parsonages throughout the Kentucky Mountain Holiness Association. He taught mathematics, science and Latin in the high school and served as dorm supervisor in the boys' dormitory. He was a wonderful man of God. He had a large scar on his face. The scar occurred at birth. He struggled over his appearance. He felt he was ugly. But for us that knew him we didn't notice the scar. The sanctifying presence of the Holy Spirit beautified his life.

The soul is the citadel of our innermost self. The conscience resides there. God wants to purge, sensitize and give us a conscience void of offense toward God and man. We will then become conscientious about our appearance, the places we go, what we read, what we listen to, what we watch and about keeping the Lord's Day holy. We will want to do nothing that grieves the heart of our Lord.

The will resides in this area. God wants to sanctify our will so that all our choices will align with His will. Thus our will and God's will become one and the same. The heart is not divided.

The affections are in this area. God wants to crucify all self love and world love. He wants for us to love Him perfectly, or completely, with all our heart, soul, mind and strength to love our neighbor as ourselves. He wants the inner motive of our heart to be love for Him. This will effect every action and reaction.

When our children were small, my wife and I were dorm supervisors in the boys dorm at Mount Carmel High School. There were a number of beautiful flower beds on the campus. We told our children not to bother the flowers, for they were not ours. They belonged to the school. One day our oldest son brought his mother a bouquet of tulips. I felt he had been disobedient and deserved a spanking. It was near Mother's Day, and we learned they had a story in Sunday School about a child that wanted to do something nice for mother on Mother's

Day, and so the child took mommy a bouquet of flowers. When I saw the motive behind what my son did, he did not get the spanking. When God sees our motive, even though our service may be cumbersome and blundersome, He is pleased when He sees that we are motivated by pure, holy love.

Our desires, appetites and passions lie in this area. God wants to purge and purify our desires and passions, so we won't want to violate His law. We won't want to take advantage of another person. Thus a young lady would feel perfectly safe in the company of such a young man. He would consider doing no wrong thing.

David prayed, "Create in me a clean heart, O God; and renew a right spirit within me." (Psalm 51:10) God wants us to have a sanctified spirit. He wants us to have a kind spirit rather than an unkind spirit, a generous spirit rather than a stingy and miserly spirit, and a forgiving spirit rather than an unforgiving spirit. He wants us to have a selfless spirit rather than a selfish and self centered spirit, a loving spirit rather than a hateful and mean spirit, and a Christlike spirit rather than an un-Christlike spirit. This can only be accomplished through God's sanctifying grace. Paul prays for the whole of our being to be sanctified through and through: spirit, soul, and body.

Fifth, entire sanctification is a PRESERVING work of grace. That which is preserved is kept sweet, not pickled or kept sour.

My mother used to make delicious strawberry preserves. She would store them where she kept her canned goods in the basement of our home. Months could pass, and the snow could fly. We could go to the shelf and get a jar of those strawberry preserves and bring it up to the kitchen table. We could take the seal off, scrape a little off the top and dig in and put some of those preserves on our toast or biscuit. It was so good. Those preserves had been kept sweet. God wants us to be kept sweet in spite of trials, criticism, misunderstanding, opposition and suffering.

Two of our good friends have gone through so much suffering. The wife had surgery for acoustic neuroma. She lay unconscious for months. They discovered a surgical sponge had been left accidentally in the incision. This caused her to suffer bacterial meningitis and a stroke. Since then she has been stricken with blindness. Her husband was in a near fatal car wreck when a lady high on drugs hit him head on. He had seventeen or more broken bones and had seventeen surgeries. This was five years ago. He now is walking with a walker. More recently their daughter and grandson died in a house fire. In spite of all they have gone through, God has kept them sweet in their spirit.

He wants to keep us sweet and blameless. The Wesley Study Bible says, "We are kept blameless before God when we do not voluntarily transgress His law. Blamelessness is preserved as we obey the new light God gives us."

Suppose your young children are fussing at the dinner table. You warn them to stop, or else they might spill the milk or break a glass. They continue, and a mess is made. Suppose another time, they are obedient, helping set the table, and a glass breaks and milk is spilt. In both cases there is fault, but only in the first is their blame. God wants us to be kept blameless.

Paul says we are to be preserved or kept blameless unto the coming of Christ. He keeps me as I keep myself in the love of Christ by continual obedience to His will. In II Timothy 1:12 Paul says, "I am persuaded that He is able to keep that which I have committed unto Him against that day." We don't have to fail and backslide. Entire sanctification is essential to being kept and to getting established in the Christian life. Paul said in Romans 5:1-2, "Therefore being justified by faith, we have peace with God through our Lord Jesus Christ: by whom also we have access by faith into this grace wherein we stand, and rejoice in hope of the glory of God."

My own life was marked by spiritual failure. I was back and forth to the altar many times. Then I experienced entire sanctification as a second work of grace and God brought an establishment into my Christian life. Jude 24 and 25 says, "Now unto Him that is able to keep you from falling, and to present you faultless before the presence of His glory with exceeding joy, to the only wise God our Savior, be glory and majesty, dominion and power, both now and ever. Amen."

Sixth, entire sanctification is an ON-GOING work of grace. I must daily keep my consecration complete. I put the unknown bundle or the unknown future on the altar when I consecrated and surrendered my all to Jesus Christ. As the contents of the unknown future surface, I must keep saying "yes" to the will of God. I must daily do God's will for me and seek His fresh anointing on my life. I must daily walk in the light as instructed in I John 1:7 where John says, "If we walk in the light, as He is in the light, we have fellowship one with another, and the blood of Jesus Christ His Son cleanseth us from all sin." I must continue to hunger for more of God. There is no place to let up and grow careless. God continues to conform us more and more into the image of His Son, Jesus Christ.

John L. Brasher was converted at age nineteen. He was called to preach, educated and pastoring in Birmingham, Alabama, when Commissioner Samuel Logan Brengle of the Salvation Army came to Birmingham and preached on entire sanctification. John Brasher went to hear him and opposed his preaching. He said, "I could argue against his doctrine, but I could not argue against his face." John Brasher met with Commissioner Brengle and poured out his heart to him as he had done to no one else. He received from Mr. Brengle the answer he did not want to hear. Mr. Brengle said, "I think entire sanctification will fix you up." At a following service John Brasher knelt between a drunkard and a harlot and died out. On a train a few days later reading A. M. Hills book "Holiness and Power", somewhere between Birmingham and Chattanooga, the Holy Spirit came. He said, "He came gently, quietly, assuringly, and with such fullness of peace I had never experienced. That was the most important experience of my life."

I. Entire sanctification is a second work of grace.
II. Entire sanctification is an instantaneous work of grace.
III. Entire sanctification is a Divine work of grace.
IV. Entire sanctification is a thorough work of grace.
V. Entire sanctification is a preserving or keeping work of grace.
VI. Entire sanctification is an on-going work of grace.

"And the very God of peace sanctify you wholly; and I pray God your whole spirit and soul and body be preserved blameless unto the coming of our Lord Jesus Christ. Faithful is He that calleth you, who also will do it" (I Thessalonians 5:23-24).

Have you experienced God's sanctifying grace in your life? God wants to make it a personal reality.

The Fullness of The Spirit
Or
Six Steps to Spirit Fullness

"And be not drunk with wine, wherein is excess; but be filled with the Spirit" (Ephesians 5:18).

The similarity of those drunk with wine and those filled with the Spirit is only on the surface. A person drunk with wine and under its control has impaired judgment. He says and does things he normally would not say and do.

A person that is filled with the Holy Spirit and under His control has improved judgment. He acts in a sane and responsible way and rejoices when under the control of the Holy Spirit.

What fills us influences us. A person that is filled with an alcoholic beverage is often said to be under the influence. He may do things for which he will later be sorry. A person filled with anger may say and do things he will later regret.

A sheriff not far from here arrested a man under the influence of alcohol. The sheriff knew the man for he had arrested him on similar charges in the past. The sheriff had befriended him and his family in times of need. So, the sheriff put hand cuffs on him in the front of his body and not behind his back. He was put in the cruiser. While in transit to the police station, the man saw a pistol on the floor of the cruiser under the front seat. He was able to get the pistol and shot and killed the sheriff. When he became sober, he did not remember what he had done and was full of regret. He said the sheriff had been kind to him, and he liked him.

If we are filled with the Holy Spirit we are influenced and controlled by the Holy Spirit. We will reflect His character and power. We will manifest the fruit of the Spirit: love, joy, peace, patience, kindness, goodness, faithfulness, gentleness and self control (Galations 5:22,23).

"Be filled with the Spirit" is a command and parallels Christ's command to His disciples in Luke 24:49 which says, "Behold I send the promise of my Father upon you; but tarry ye in the city of Jerusalem, until ye be endued with power from on high."

While on the Mount of Olives, prior to His ascension, Christ commanded His disciples in Acts 1:4,5 to, "Wait for the promise of the Father, which ye have heard of me. For John truly baptized with water; but ye shall be baptized with the Holy Ghost not many days hence." When this promise was fulfilled on the day of Pentecost we read in Acts 2:2; "Suddenly," in a moment in time, "They were all filled with the Holy Ghost" (Acts 2:4). Spirit fullness became a personal reality in an instantaneous crisis moment.

Peter explained in Acts 2:39 that this promise of the Spirit's fullness was not just for the120 at Pentecost. He said, "The promise is unto you and your children, and to all that are afar off, even as many as the Lord our God shall call." Spirit fullness is for all believers.

When Peter explained at the council in Jerusalem that the Gentiles received the Holy Spirit the same way the Jews received the Holy Spirit, he said in Acts 15:9 that their hearts were purified by faith.

The two essential elements of Pentecost are purity and power. We must be emptied of self, before we can be filled with the Spirit. Purity always precedes power.

J. Gregory Mantle said, "It is one thing to have the Spirit; it is quite another to be filled with the Spirit. You may be full as the white hot iron is full of fire. It is cold, hard and black. You put it in the fire, and the fire enters into it, and soon the fire changes its color. That white-hot iron is now possessed, inter-penetrated by the fire within it." Even so we can be filled, possessed and inner-penetrated by the fire of the Holy Spirit. John the Baptist in Matthew 3:11 said, "I indeed baptize you with water unto repentance: but He that cometh after me is mightier than I, whose shoes I am not worthy to bear: He shall baptize you with the Holy Ghost and with fire."

Every born again Christian receives the Holy Spirit. Paul said in Romans 5:5 that, "The love of God is shed abroad in our hearts by the Holy Spirit which is given unto us." In Romans 8:9b Paul said, "If any man have not the Spirit of Christ, he is none of His." Jesus said in John 14:16,17, "And I will pray the Father, and He shall give you another Comforter, that He may abide with you for ever. Even the Spirit of truth; whom the world (the unregenerated world) cannot receive, because it seeth Him not, neither knoweth Him: but ye know Him; for He dwelleth with you (this is the experience of every born again believer), and shall be in you (Jesus pointed to a fullness of the Spirit they were to experience at Pentecost)."

The Apostle Paul appealed to Christians in Romans 12:1 to present themselves as living sacrifices. He said, "I beseech you therefore, brethren, by the mercies of God, that ye present your bodies a living sacrifice, holy, acceptable unto God, which is your reasonable service." Only born again believers can do this. The sinner needs forgiveness and new life in Christ. It is then he can present himself a living sacrifice to God that he might be filled with the Holy Spirit.

I wish to suggest six steps to Spirit fullness.

  I. ASSURANCE of personal salvation
 II. ACKNOWLEDGEMENT of the need of the Spirit's fullness
III. APPETITE for the Spirit's fullness
IV. ABANDONMENT of self to the will of God
 V. ASKING for the fullness of the Spirit
VI. APPROPRIATING by faith the fullness of the Spirit

One must have a clear witness and ASSURANCE that he is a born again Christian to be a candidate for the fullness of the Holy Spirit. God does not fill with His Spirit unsaved people or anyone living in known sin and disobedience to His commands. He does not empower with His Spirit those living in rebellion to the known will of God. Sin must be openly confessed, repented of, forsaken and forgiven. Sinful living must cease, and we must be walking in all the light. There must be a clear witness and evidence that we have been born of the Spirit to qualify for the fullness of the Spirit.

The second step to Spirit fullness is ACKNOWLEDGEMENT of the need. Saved people sooner or later discover they have a deeper need. It is better that they discover it sooner, rather than later. The Word of God reveals that need, and human experience confirms it.

Dr. Lela G. McConnell was the founder of the Kentucky Mountain Holiness Association. As a student at Mount Carmel High School and the Kentucky Mountain Bible Institute, I sang in a male quartet and had the privilege of traveling many miles with her as she represented the Kentucky Mountain Holiness Association. I heard her testimony many times. She told of how she was converted at age thirteen in a revival meeting in the Honey Brook, Pennsylvania, Methodist Church. She loved the Lord, read her Bible, prayed, regularly attended church and helped the pastor in any way she could. After graduating from high school, at age eighteen, she began teaching school in a one room school house. This was common in those days. Her mother had been a school teacher, and her sister was a school teacher. Her mother instructed her and her sister to keep order in the school room. She endeavored to do that. One day a boy misbehaved, and she sought to correct him. He didn't correct his behavior. She said, "I flew at him like a cat at a mouse. I wiped up the floor with him. The tragedy was that I was white with anger." That evening she went to her boarding house and fell across her bed. She asked the Lord to forgive her, not for the discipline, but for getting angry. She apologized to the student for getting angry and wrote to a friend asking where she could get more religion. She said, "I need it and need it fast." Her friend told her of a holiness camp meeting in Delanco, New Jersey, where five old fashioned Methodist preachers were preaching the message of entire sanctification and the fullness of the Holy Spirit. She went to that camp meeting, and it was there she experienced Spirit fullness. She had to first acknowledge her need before she became a seeker for the fullness of the Spirit. We don't call for the fire department unless the house is on fire. We have to realize the need.

Dr. Warren McIntyre told of a young girl that got gloriously saved. Her pastor began to preach on the need of a pure heart. The young woman came to her pastor and said, "I don't sense the need of a pure heart. I've been so happy since I got saved." The pastor was wise and directed her to Psalm 139:23,24 which says, "Search me, O God, and know my heart: try me, and know my thoughts: and see if there be any wicked way in me, and lead me in the way everlasting." He encouraged her to make this her prayer in her private prayer time. She took the challenge and took paper and pencil along to write down anything the Holy Spirit revealed to her that would show her the need for a pure heart. The Holy Spirit revealed to her twelve things. He showed her that she had a lack of love for secret prayer. She tended to be jealous of others. She had a tendency to be proud of her abilities. She would often pout if she didn't get her way. She would often be unduly critical of others. The Holy Spirit further revealed that she had a heart fear of the judgment. She had to acknowledge her need of heart purity and the fullness of the Spirit before she became a seeker.

Someone may say, "I know I'm saved, but I've never sensed the need of the fullness of the Holy Spirit." Ask God to search your heart. Jeremiah 17:9 says, "The heart is deceitful above all things, and desperately wicked; who can know it?" God alone knows our hearts. Ask Him to give you a guided tour of your own heart. It may help to pray the prayer of Psalm 139:23,24, and take paper and pencil with you to write down what the Holy Spirit shows you.   We then need to honestly confess our heart need. Name to God the things the Holy Spirit reveals. Perhaps there have been failures, compromise, defeats, prejudice, wrong attitudes, unforgiveness, pride, hate, lust, jealousy, self centeredness, or carnal anger among other things that have been displeasing to God.

Ask God to deal with your heart and cleanse it from all carnal traits. You can rejoice that He has made provision to do just that. In Hebrews 13:12 we read, "Wherefore Jesus also, that He might sanctify the people with His own blood, suffered without the gate." Jesus prayed in John 17:17, "Sanctify them through Thy truth; Thy Word is truth." In John 17:20, Jesus said, "Neither pray I for these (disciples) alone, but for them also which shall believe on me through their word." This includes every believer that has ever lived and ever will live. In I John 1:7 John said, "But if we walk in the light, as He is in the light, we have fellowship one with another, and the blood of Jesus Christ His Son cleanseth us from all sin." In Acts 2:39 Peter said, "For the promise is unto you, and to your children, and to all who are afar off, even as many as the Lord our God shall call."

The third step to Spirit fullness is APPETITE. God responds to soul hunger and soul thirst. Isaiah writes in Isaiah 55:1, "Ho, everyone that thirsteth, come ye to the waters." In Isaiah 44:3 God says, "I will pour water upon him that is thirsty, and floods upon the dry ground: I will pour my Spirit upon thy seed, and my blessing upon thine offspring." Jesus said in Matthew 5:6, "Blessed are they which do hunger and thirst after righteousness: for they shall be filled." In John 7:37-39 Jesus spoke again saying, "If any man thirst, let him come unto me and drink. He that believeth on me, as the Scripture hath said, out of his belly shall flow rivers of living water. But this spake He of the Spirit."

Water is symbolic of the Holy Spirit. You must wholeheartedly desire the fullness of the Spirit or you will not be filled with the Spirit. If you are content to go without the fullness of the Spirit, you will not be filled with the Spirit. No one has ever been filled with the Spirit who felt he could get along without that fullness. God spoke in Jeremiah 29:13 and said, "Ye shall seek Me, and find Me, when ye shall search for Me with all your heart."

There are two major reasons for not knowing the fullness of the Spirit. The individual does not seek it with all the heart or make a full surrender to the whole will of God.

George Fox, founder of the Society of Friends, was born again at age eleven. At age twenty-three he hungered and thirsted for a deeper experience with God. A new enduement of power came upon him. From that time forward he was mightily used of God.

The story is told of a man who was seeking the fullness of the Spirit. He asked a friend where he might find this fullness. The friend told him there was a good place down the road. They went a short distance, and he asked how much farther it was. The answer was that it was not much farther. They went a short distance; again he asked the same question and received the same answer. They walked on, and finally the man said, "I can't wait any longer." His friend said, "This is the place." When we get so hungry that we can't wait any longer we have come to the place where we can know the fullness of the Holy Spirit.

The fourth step to Spirit fullness is the ABANDONMENT of self to the whole will of God. There must be a total surrender to the lordship of Christ before anyone can know the fullness of the Holy Spirit. The Apostle Paul calls believers to that surrender in Romans 12:1 where he says, "I beseech you therefore brethren, by the mercies of God, that you present your bodies a living sacrifice, holy, acceptable unto God, which is your reasonable service (or no more than you ought to do)." It is giving to God all you are and all you ever will be. It is giving to God all you have and ever will have. It is for all time and all eternity and all means ALL.

It is the crucifixion of the carnal self life. Paul writes in Galations 2:20, "I am crucified with Christ: nevertheless I live; yet not I, but Christ liveth in me: and the life which I how live in the flesh I live by the faith of the Son of God, who loved me, and gave Himself for me." Again Paul writes in Romans 6:11-13, "Likewise reckon ye also yourselves to be dead indeed unto sin, but alive unto God through Jesus Christ our Lord. Let not sin (the sin nature) therefore reign in your mortal body, that ye should obey it in the lusts thereof. Neither yield ye your members as instruments of unrighteousness unto sin: but yield yourselves unto God, as those that are alive from the dead, and your members as instruments of righteousness unto God."

This is the emptying that precedes the filling. It is the surrender of all - known and unknown. It is the total abandonment of my plans, ambitions, and will to God's will.

Think of your life as a check-book where you sign all the checks in advance and let God fill in the blanks. All is surrendered to Him. It is an eternal yes to God and His will. It is the big YES that will be followed by a lot of smaller yeses as the contents of the unknown future are revealed. You are all God's. He is Lord, and you gladly submit and obey. Fanny Crosby wrote, "Perfect submission, all is at rest. I in my Savior am happy and blest."

Dr. Walter Wilson was converted in his teens. Eighteen years later he was challenged to make a full surrender of his life to Christ. He lay on the carpet in his study and made a detailed and absolute surrender. He testified, "With regard to my experience with the Holy Spirit, I may say that the transformation in my own life on January 14, 1914, was greater, much greater than the change which took place when I was saved December 21, 1896."

The smartest thing that Eldon Neihof ever did was to surrender his life completely to Jesus Christ on March 9, 1952. That is truly the smartest thing that anyone can ever do.

The fifth step to Spirit fullness is to ASK for the fullness of the Holy Spirit. Jesus said in Luke 11:13, "If ye then being evil (earthly), know how to give good gifts unto your children: how much more shall your heavenly Father give the Holy Spirit to them that ask Him." Asking and receiving need not take long for God is always ready to fulfill His promise. Paul writes in I Thessalonians 5:24, "Faithful is He that calleth you, who also will do it."

From God's standpoint there need be no waiting. He is always ready to fulfill His promise. From our standpoint God sometimes blesses a period of waiting. The disciples waited ten days. During that time the Holy Spirit searched their hearts. Their heart hunger was deepened. The Holy Spirit revealed new depths of spiritual need. It may have been a needed apology, a restitution, or a relationship that needed to be repaired. Peter may have needed to apologize to the other disciples for lording it over them. They may have resented Peter and needed to ask his forgiveness. During that ten day waiting period they got in one accord.

Hudson Taylor, the missionary, said, "Should we not do well to suspend our present operations and give ourselves to humiliation and prayer for nothing less than to be filled with the Spirit, and made channels through which He shall work with resistless power?"

We must ask definitely for the fullness of the Holy Spirit.

The sixth and final step to Spirit fullness is to APPROPRIATE or receive by faith the promised fullness of the Holy Spirit. The fullness of the Spirit can only be received by faith by the born again Child of God. You don't have to become more worthy by good works. You don't have to prove yourself through self-discipline or prolonged periods of fasting and prayer. The fullness of the Spirit is not received by works but by faith alone. In Acts 15:8,9 Peter testified, "And God, which knoweth the hearts, bare them witness, giving them the Holy Ghost, even as He did unto us; and put no difference between us and them (Jew and Gentile), purifying their hearts by faith." God always purifies and empowers when He fills with His Spirit, and we appropriate or receive by simple faith.

A. J. Gordon said, "It seems clear from the Scriptures that it is still the duty and privilege of believers to receive the Holy Spirit by a conscious, definite act of appropriating faith. It is as sinners that we accept Christ (by faith) for our justification, but it is as sons that we accept the Spirit (by faith) for our sanctification."

Nothing is more simple. When electric lines are installed and connected to the power supply, even a child can turn on lights by touching a switch. Even so, when we have prepared our hearts by getting genuinely converted, acknowledging our need, hungering for all of God, surrendering totally to God, asking definitely, all we have to do is touch God by simple faith.

The filling is instantaneous. The moment your faith takes hold, He fills.

D. L. Moody had been greatly used of God. Two humble Free Methodist ladies prayed faithfully for him. At the close of a service they would say, "We have been praying for you." He would reply, "Why don't you pray for the people?"   They answered, "Because you need the power of the Spirit." He thought he had power. He had the largest congregation in Chicago and there were many conversions.

One day Mr. Moody said to these ladies, "I wish you would tell me what you mean." They told him about the definite infilling of the Holy Spirit. Shortly thereafter their prayers were answered. Dr. R. A. Torrey described what happened. "The power of God fell upon him as he walked up the street, and he had to hurry to the house of a friend and ask that he might have a room by himself, and in that room he stayed for hours; and the Holy Ghost came upon him filling his soul with such joy that at last he had to ask God to withhold His hand, lest he die on the spot from the joy. He went out from that place with the power of the Holy Ghost upon him."

Mr. Moody testified, "The sermons were not different; I did not present new truth; and yet hundreds were converted. I would not be placed back where I was before that blessed experience if you should give me all the world."

At his funeral Dr. C. I. Scofield said, "One reason God used Moody was, he was baptized with the Holy Spirit and he knew that he was. It was to him as definite experience as his conversion."

To be filled with the spirit is not an option. It is a necessity. It is absolutely necessary for victorious living and fruitful service. It is intended for all, needed by all and available to all believers.

There is one initial filling of the Holy Spirit. There are many reanointings and fresh infillings. "Be filled with the Spirit" is a command and means get filled and keep filled, or be continually filled with the Spirit.

I have mentioned six steps to Spirit fullness.

I. ASSURANCE you're saved
II. ACKNOWLEDGEMENT of need
III. APPETITE
IV. ABANDONMENT of self
V. ASKING definitely
VI. APPROPRIATING (receiving) by faith

If you will take these simple steps you can know the reality of the fullness of the Holy Spirit in your heart and life today.

Distinctions In The Sanctified Life

I Thessalonians 3:12,13

The Apostle Paul was greatly concerned that Christians would get established. He recognized that holiness is a great asset to that end. When entirely sanctified, carnal hindrances are removed, and spiritual growth can then be at its best. The inner opposition to God's will and government has been removed. Our will is to do God's will. We love God with all our hearts and hunger to be more like Him.

However, there are some necessary distinctions that will aid us in our spiritual development and growth.

One such distinction is between inbred sin and actual sin or between the nature of sin and the practice of sin or between sin inherited and sin committed.

Inbred sin is an inherited tendency to do wrong which we received from fallen Adam. It is a twist, a warp, or a bent in our nature toward evil. It is a mindedness away from God and toward sin. It is a tendency to love self rather than to love God and to want our way instead of God's way. David said in Psalm 51:5, "Behold I was shapen in iniquity; and in sin did my mother conceive me." Inbred sin is an inner self centeredness that disturbs the inner life and compromises the outer life. It poisons our self interests and directs our goals and values to selfish ends.

Actual sin is a wilful act of disobedience to the will and law of God. In I John 3:4 John says, "Sin is the transgression of the law." Sin is lawlessness. It is an act of disregard for God's law and comes from a lawless condition within the heart of man called the carnal mind. The Apostle Paul writes in Romans 8:7 that, "The carnal mind is enmity against God: for it is not subject to the law of God, neither indeed can be."

Inbred sin is the root of the sin problem while actual committed sin is the fruit. Inbred sin is the cause while actual sin is the effect.

A second distinction we need to make is between mistakes and sins. A mistake is an unintentional violation which does not result in guilt and condemnation. It may be caused by a lack of knowledge or human weakness. A sin is a known, volitional, wilful wrong that does result in guilt and condemnation.

Suppose I'm a clerk in a store. You make some purchases in my store and hand me a fifty dollar bill to pay for your purchases. In giving you your change I short change you five dollars. You leave the store without noticing the missing five dollars. I discovered the error after you had left the store. I feel badly about it and purpose to repay you at the first opportunity, and I do. We recognize that this would be a mistake and not a sin. But suppose you make the same purchases and in giving you your change I purposely withhold five dollars. You do not miss it. I keep the money and spend it. This would not be a mistake. It would be an intentional wrong. It would be a wilful and known sin.

John Wesley said, "Sin properly so called is the wilful violation of a known law." A mistake comes from the head; a sin comes from the heart. A mistake is not a sin, and a sin is not a mistake. Mistakes need to be corrected and apologized for but do not require repentance as does sin. Dr. Daniel Steele said, "A thousand mistakes are consistent with perfect love but not one sin." Only three classes never make mistakes: the unborn, the dead and those who never did anything.

Another distinction needs to be made between humanity and carnality. Humanity, as pertains to a sanctified Christian, consists of our original human nature, free from the carnal mind, but still marred and hindered by infirmities and weaknesses which are the direct consequence of the fall.

Humanity consists of the essential elements of human personality, including God given gifts, desires and drives. The power of choice, the power of reason, curiosity, appetite for food, the desire for friendship including the desire for the opposite sex are all God given. These are not sinful and wrong. They are not removed when entirely sanctified. However, they need to be disciplined and used the way God intended, or they could lead to sin.

It is not wrong to get hungry. It is wrong to steal food to satisfy the hunger. It is not wrong to get thirsty. It is wrong to break into a vending machine to get something to drink. It is not wrong to be attracted to the opposite sex. It is wrong to lust and to satisfy this God given desire outside of marriage.

Humanity includes human limitations. We may have limited physical strength. Some have greater mental capacities than others. Our intelligent quotient (IQ) may differ greatly than that of others. We understand at differing levels. We have limited abilities, talents and gifts.

Humanity includes different temperaments or natural ways of acting and reacting. Some are quick, and others are slow. Some are like the work horse and others like the race horse. Some are quiet, while others are loud. Some are outgoing, while others are retiring. One may be an extrovert, while another is an introvert.

Humanity includes different personalities which make for variety and richness. However, these different personalities may make for stress, incompatibility and misunderstanding in human relations.

Humanity includes infirmities such as weariness, faulty memories, emotional and psychological hangups. These hangups may have resulted from physical, emotional and sexual abuse. They may require professional counseling.

Carnality consists of self love, pride, jealousy, envy, rebellion, self centeredness and wanting our own way. Carnality can be cleansed or crucified. The Apostle Paul wrote in Romans 6:6, "Knowing this, that our old man (the carnal mind) is (present tense) crucified (put to death) with Him (Christ), that the body of sin (the carnal mind) might be destroyed (not suppressed), that henceforth we should not serve sin."

For the self ego to be crucified with Christ does not mean its extinction. That would end the person. It means the ego is dead to its carnal claim to self rule. A crucified self never says, "I want my own way" or demands its own rights. It means self is yielded, surrendered and submitted to the will of God. It is cleansed from self centeredness. Paul testifies in Galations 2:20 and says, "I (the self centered carnal I) am crucified with Christ; nevertheless I (the human I) live; yet not I (the carnal I), but Christ liveth in me: and the life I now live in the flesh (this body) I live by the faith of the Son of God, who loved me, and gave Himself for me."

Humanity needs to be disciplined, directed and sometimes modified. Paul said, "I keep my body under." Paul is saying that he rules his body and does not let his human drives rule him.

God, the Holy Spirit, is concerned for holy character. He takes life's experiences, shocks, blows, sorrows, sufferings, unpleasant people and situations and uses them as sandpaper to knock off the rough edges of our personalities and develop us more and more into the likeness of Christ. He wants us to be ourselves in the Lord. He wants us totally surrendered to Him and cleansed from the carnal mind. He further wants to empower us with the Holy Spirit and make us His witnesses in the world.

Yet another distinction that will help us in our spiritual development is the distinction between purity and maturity. Purity involves forgiveness from the guilt of committed sin, followed by cleansing from the nature of sin. Purity speaks of undivided devotion to God alone. It speaks of single mindedness, rather than double mindedness. It is the cure for the disposition to serve both God and the world. It is to be cleansed from hate, lust, bitterness, pride, and all carnal traits. It is to be filled with Divine love. Our love is made perfect. It is no longer mixed with love of self and love of the world. We love God with all our heart, soul, mind and strength. It is when inward preferences and outward profession match. I don't have to pretend and put on something I am not.

Maturity is the gradual result of living. It is the product of growing up physically and spiritually. It is the product of battles fought, temptations resisted, obstacles overcome, problems solved and wounds healed. It is stability that holds us steady in difficult times. It is skill in living the Christian life. It is where we become more discerning, gain more poise in times of turmoil and acquire greater depths in Bible knowledge and doctrine. It is gaining a greater understanding of things that really matter and being able to work out our own salvation into consistent, ethical practice.

Maturity is not flawless for "We have this treasure in earthen vessels." The pure, but immature, may have areas that have not been the subject of light. The pure, but immature, may have ethical blind spots and do things inconsistent with holy living and be unaware of it. The pure, but immature, may not be culturally refined. It may take years, but the Holy Spirit will gradually change us or leave us. We either grow, or we die. Oswald Chambers said, "Slovenliness is an insult to the Holy Spirit." God wants to make us Christian ladies and gentlemen. He does not bless rudeness and crudeness. He does bless kindness, courtesy and loving gracious concern for others.

Purity happens in an instant; maturity takes a lifetime. Mature Christians need to exercise great patience with those who are younger in the faith and less mature. Older Christians need to come alongside younger Christians to mentor, encourage and aid them in the maturing process.

It is further essential to distinguish between crisis and process in Christian experience. The new birth is the first crisis. This is holiness begun. In the new birth sins are forgiven, guilt is removed, and we become new creatures in Christ Jesus. We are born of the Spirit. The Holy Spirit enables us to live victoriously over known wilful sin. John writes in I John 3:9, "Whosoever is born of God doth not commit sin; for His seed remaineth in him: and he cannot sin, because he is born of God." John says we cannot be sinning and be a born again Christian at the same time.

Entire sanctification is a second crisis in Christian experience. It is then that we are cleansed instantaneously from inherited sin or the carnal mind. This is followed or accompanied by the empowering of the Holy Spirit. Jesus said to the disciples in Acts 1:8, "Ye shall receive power, after that the Holy Ghost is come upon you: and ye shall be witnesses unto me both in Jerusalem, and in all Judea, and in Samaria, and unto the uttermost part of the earth." The empowering of the Holy Spirit is absolutely necessary for victorious living and fruitful service.

Beyond these two definite crisis experiences of the new birth and entire sanctification as a second work of God's grace, there is progressive sanctification. This is a never ending process of walking in light, learning new truth from God's Word and the fashioning of the personality into ever-increasing more Christlikeness. The Apostle Paul writes in Romans 8:29 and says, "For whom He did foreknow, He also did predestinate to be conformed to the image of His Son, that He might be the first born among many brethren." The conforming into the likeness of Christ involves self discipline and learning. One excellent way to learn is to read the biographies of great holiness people, as well as the writings of great holiness writers. It includes a meaningful prayer life and regular exposure to God's Word. Witnessing, sensitivity to the checks and guidance of the Holy Spirit are all important. Walking in new light, attendance to the means of grace such as regular devotions, tithing and consistent church attendance are essential. There is an after work as well as an altar work. This is an unending, ongoing and life long process. It is a wonderful journey that gets richer along the way.

Another distinction is between the ethical and unethical in Christian living. Ethics refer to moral principles and practices. If we profess to be Christians, we have a responsibility to practice the highest standards of Christian conduct. In I Peter 1:15 Peter tells us, "But as He which hath called you is holy, so be ye holy in all manner of conversation (conduct or life style)."

In James 3:17 James tells us that a Christian is, "Easy to be entreated." He is teachable. If he becomes aware that what he is doing is wrong he ceases to do it. If he becomes aware that what he is doing is a stumbling block to someone else he is willing to cease doing it.

A Christian person is conscientious, and if not, he is a fake. He is conscientious about his work and does an honest day's work for his wage. He is conscientious about his word. He keeps his word. He is conscientious about his obligations and pays his bills on time. He is conscientious about his stewardship. He honors God with his talents, time and resources. He is conscientious about his citizenship and obeys the law. He is conscientious about his appearance. Christians adorn themselves with modesty of apparel that is Christ honoring. They are conscientious and careful to conduct themselves appropriately in relating to the opposite sex. They are careful in the use of the television and the internet.

They are concerned about pleasing the Lord in all things and are further concerned about their influence on others.
They do not want to be a stumbling block to another person and want their lives to be Christ honoring in all things.

Still in another area we need to distinguish between natural timidity and carnal fear. In I John 4:18b we read, "Perfect love casteth our fear." But we must recognize that perfect love does not cast out all fear. The Bible recognizes different kinds of fear. Filial fear is the fear of an obedient child that wants to please his parents. Reverential fear causes us to stand in reverence and awe in God's presence. The Psalmist said in Psalm 111:10, "The fear of the Lord is the beginning of wisdom." It causes us to want to please Him and not grieve Him because we love Him. Constitutional fear is necessary for the preservation of the race. This speaks of fear of danger. When we see a sign that says "High Voltage, Stay Out", we ought to have enough sense to stay out. When we see a red light flashing we ought to have sense enough to stop. Constitutional fear means we stay away from dangerous beasts, poisonous snakes and other dangers.

Carnal fear is slavish or paralyzing fear that renders us helpless to do God's will. It manifests itself in man fear. A dear man that was an outstanding holiness preacher testified to being converted and at the same time being called to preach. For ten years he ran from that call and did not preach. After ten years he got gloriously sanctified. God delivered him from carnal man fear, and he became a powerful holiness preacher. Carnal fear ties us in knots and keeps us from testifying, teaching a Sunday School class, preaching and going to the mission field. Perfect love will cast out carnal fear. God can deliver from carnal fear, but we will, without doubt, still have filial fear, reverential fear and constitutional fear.

Dr. T. M. Anderson said, "Many sanctified people suffer from timidity." Some people are naturally bold and others are naturally timid. No amount of seeking at the altar can deliver from natural timidity. It is best overcome by trusting God and doing the thing that is difficult to do.

When I was asked to serve as academic dean at the Kentucky Mountain Bible Institute, I had a lot of fears. These fears made me wonder and concerned about my relationship to the Lord. I read what the Apostle Paul wrote to the church at Corinth in I Corinthians 2:3 where he said, "I was with you in weakness and in fear, and in much trembling." This made me feel that I was in pretty good company. My heart was further encouraged by the words of Isaiah in Isaiah 41:10 where he wrote, "Fear thou not; for I am with thee: be not dismayed; for I am thy God I will strengthen thee; yea, I will help thee; yea, I will uphold thee with the right hand of my righteousness."

I will confess that there have been many times when I have stood before a large congregation to preach and my knees got friendly. One said to the other, "Let's shake."

A final distinction is between faith and feeling. Feelings fluctuate. We have mountains and valleys emotionally. Feelings are like the roller coaster or the stock market. They are up and down. Feelings do not indicate the amount of grace we enjoy. When fiery trials, illness, disaster, temptation, or death comes we don't usually feel very blessed. It has been said that feelings depend on what you look at. You can look at others with their limitations, faults and hypocrisies, and you won't feel much blessing. If you do that, the devil will always lend you his magnifying glass to magnify them way out of proportion. You can look at yourself. Occasional inventory may be a good thing, but this can be overdone. None of us get much blessing from looking at ourselves. On the other hand you can look to Jesus. The evangelist, C. W. Ruth, once said, "If you want to be defeated look behind; if you want to be dismayed look ahead; if you want to be miserable look at yourself; and if you want to be happy look to Jesus."

Feeling occurs one time in the Bible. Faith occurs three hundred times. One man went by feeling, and he blessed the wrong boy. Issac blessed Jacob instead of Essau.

We are saved by faith, sanctified by faith and walk by faith. Our relationship with Jesus Christ does not depend on our feeling; it entirely depends on our faith.

In Hebrews 10:23 and 35 the Hebrew writer states, "Let us hold fast the profession of our faith without wavering (for He is faithful that promised). Cast not away your confidence, which hath great recompense of reward." The Apostle Peter said in II Peter 3:18, "But grow in grace, and in the knowledge of our Lord and Savior Jesus Christ. To Him be glory now and forever."

The Holy Spirit

John 16:5-16

Our total salvation is the work of the Holy Spirit. All that is ours in redemption we receive through the faithful working of the Holy Spirit.

John Wesley said, "I believe in the infinite and eternal spirit of God, equal with the Father and the Son, to be not only perfectly holy in Himself, but the immediate cause of all holiness in us; enlightening our understandings, rectifying our wills and affections, renewing our natures, uniting our persons to Christ, purifying and sanctifying our souls and bodies, to a full and eternal enjoyment of God."

God the Father planned our salvation. God the Son provided it, and God the Holy Spirit perfects it and makes it experientially real in our hearts and lives.

There are three things I wish to address about the Holy Spirit.

I. The operation of the Holy Spirit

II. The offending of the Holy Spirit

III. The obeying of the Holy Spirit

One operation of the Holy Spirit is conviction. Jesus said in John 16:8, "And when He (the Holy Spirit) is come, He will reprove (convict and convince) the world of sin, and of righteousness, and of judgment." The Holy Spirit convicts the unsaved world of the fact that without Christ as our Savior we are all sinners, unrighteous and judgment bound. In Genesis 6:3, "The Lord said, my Spirit shall not always strive with man." In Isaiah 55:6 the prophet said, "Seek ye the Lord while He may be found, call ye upon Him while He is near." I was eight years of age the first time I can recall the Holy Spirit convicting and drawing upon my heart. I was in a revival meeting in my home church. When the altar call was given, I immediately stepped out and went to the altar. That night the Lord saved me. It was a very real experience, and I will never forget it. I'm so thankful I did not resist the Holy Spirit. It is so important that we respond to the convicting and drawing of the

Holy Spirit when He speaks.

The Holy Spirit not only convicts sinners; He also convicts saints of wrong attitudes and unkind, harsh, hurtful words. At age seventeen, a junior in a Christian high school, the Lord sanctified me wholly. The following summer I was home working in my father's place of business. His partner accused me of doing something I had not done. I immediately flew to my own defense and let him know I had not done it. I was right in what I said, but I was wrong in the way I said it. I was harsh and unkind. Immediately the Holy Spirit reproved and convicted me. My peace was disturbed. The Holy Spirit whispered, "That was unkind. You need to apologize to that man." Another voice spoke to me and said, "He's a sinner man. He would not understand. Just let it go." I had a short prayer meeting on the spot. I said, "Lord, I've started for heaven, and I don't want to let one thing stand in my way." I met that man and told him I didn't do what he accused me of doing, but I was harsh and unkind in the way I answered him. I asked him to forgive me, and my peace was restored. The songbird began to sing once again in my soul. I had been obedient to the reproof of the Holy Spirit.

Another operation of the Holy Spirit is that He regenerates us. The Apostle Paul said in Titus 3:5, "Not by works of righteousness which we have done, but according to His mercy He saved us, by the washing of regeneration, and renewing of the Holy Spirit." We repent and trust Christ for the forgiveness of our sins. He resurrects us from spiritual death to spiritual life. The Holy Spirit imparts spiritual life and makes us new creatures in Christ. In that moment He pardons us, justifies us, and adopts us into His family. He washes away our sins and puts them in the sea of His forgetfulness. He writes our names in the Lamb's book of life. We are born of the Spirit. Without the Holy Spirit there is no new birth. It is His work.

In I Corinthians 6:11 we read, "Ye are sanctified ... by the Spirit of our God." Jesus said in John 14:16-17, "I will pray the Father, and He shall give you another comforter, that He may abide with you forever; even the Spirit of truth; whom the world (the unsaved world) cannot receive, because it seeth Him not, neither knoweth Him: but ye know Him; for He dwelleth with you, and shall be in you." Jesus was pointing to Pentecost. He was speaking of a fullness of the Spirit. The Holy Spirit is with us when we are born of the Spirit. He wants us to know the fullness of the Spirit in entire sanctification. Sanctification involves consecration on our part. Sanctification involves cleansing on God's part. That which God cleanses He fills and empowers. Spiritual success is possible only when the Spirit cleanses and the Spirit empowers. Jesus said in Acts 1:8, "Ye shall receive power, after that the Holy Ghost is come upon you."

Paul writes in Romans 8:16 and says, "The Spirit itself (Himself) beareth witness with our spirit, that we are the children of God." There is the direct witness of the Spirit and the indirect witness of the Holy Spirit. John Wesley said that the direct witness of the Holy Spirit is, "An inward impression on the souls of believers, whereby the Spirit of God directly testifies to their spirit that they are the children of God." John Wesley was converted on May 24, 1738, and testified, "About a quarter before nine, while he (Peter Bolar) was describing the change which God works in the heart through faith in Christ, I felt my heart strangely warmed. I felt I did trust Christ, Christ alone, for salvation; and an assurance was given me that He had taken away my sins, even mine, and saved me from the law of sin and death." The old timers talked much about a heartfelt religion. Fanny Crosby wrote, "Blessed assurance, Jesus is mine." It stands to reason that if you could have salvation and not know it; you could lose it and not know it.

There is also the indirect witness of the Spirit. This is the fruit of the Spirit. Paul writes in Galatians 5:22,23 that, "The fruit of the Spirit is love, joy, peace, longsuffering, gentleness (kindness), goodness (genuineness), faith (faithfulness), meekness (submissiveness), temperance (self control): against such there is no law." The direct witness must precede the indirect witness for it takes time for fruit to mature.

In John 16:13 Jesus tells us, "Howbeit when He, the Spirit of truth, is come, He will guide you into all truth." Jesus speaks of the Holy Spirit as the Spirit of truth. He never guides into error and false doctrine. He always guides into truth. You can trust the Holy Spirit to guide you. He is the conserver of orthodoxy.

He often guides directly as He did in the case of Saul (Paul) and Barnabas recorded in Acts 13:2, "The Holy Ghost said, separate unto me Barnabas and Saul for the work whereunto I have called them." Paul and Barnabas were happy in the work of the church at Antioch of Syria. God was blessing, and the church was growing. Then God said, "I want you to leave and go on a missionary journey." God was calling them into their life's vocation. He wanted them to be missionaries. When I was fifteen years of age God spoke to me and said, "I want you to preach my gospel." God was guiding me into my life's vocation. God has a plan for every life and desires to guide us into our life work.

At times He guides us through godly people. Solomon wrote in Proverbs 11:14 that, "In the multitude of counselors there is safety." I am not a self-made person. God used my parents, pastors, teachers, evangelists and others to guide me. How grateful I am for these godly people that have contributed to my life.

Sometimes God guides us by closing doors and restraining us. The Apostle Paul was on his second missionary journey. He was revisting churches he had established on his first missionary journey. He wanted to go into Asia, a province of Asia Minor, but Paul was restrained. We read about it in Acts 16:6,7 where it says,."They were forbidden of the Holy Ghost to preach the word in Asia ... They assayed to go into Bithynia: but the Spirit suffered them not."

On this same missionary journey Paul went to Troas. It was there he had a vision in the night. In that vision he saw a man from Macedonia saying, "Come over into Macedonia and help us" (Acts 16:9). Paul was constrained by the Holy Spirit to cross the Agean Sea and take the Gospel to Phillippi, Thessalonica and elsewhere. He took the gospel into Europe, and eventually it came to us.

The Holy Spirit guides by the Word of God. He never guides contrary to the Holy Scriptures. The Bible is His infallible guide book.

Often the Holy Spirit guides by an inner peace. Paul writes in Colossians 3:15, "Let the peace of God rule (arbitrate, judge, settle all questions) in your hearts." Let the peace of God be like the umpire at the ball game and tell you what is a ball and what is a strike. Let it be like the judge on the bench and make the final decision. In other words, if the thing you are considering disturbs your peace, don't do it. Follow the way of peace.

Another operation of the Holy Spirit is to teach us. Jesus said in John 14:26, "He (the Holy Spirit) shall teach you all things." He teaches the things of Christ. Jesus said in John 16:13b,14, "He (the Holy Spirit) shall not speak of Himself; but whatsoever He shall hear, that shall He speak: and He will shew you things to come. He shall glorify me: for He shall receive of mine, and shall shew it unto you." The Holy Spirit teaches us the things of Christ. He lifts up Christ.

In Romans 8:26b Paul says, "The Spirit itself (Himself) maketh intercession for us." Many times the burden is so heavy we find it difficult to put it into words. The Holy Spirit interprets our tears and our groans and intercedes in our behalf.

Paul further states in Romans 8:26 that, "He (the Holy Spirit) helpeth our infirmities (weaknesses)." In the devotional book, HOLINESS AND HIGH COUNTRY, I read, "Because of human limitations, sanctified Christians often fall short of a perfect manifestation of the Spirit of love that God has put into our hearts. These infirmities are not sin. Because of ignorance, not understanding all the facts, we may do the wrong thing. Through weakness ... we may fall short in our performance. Neither is intentional and therefore does not bring guilt. It does bring humiliation and regret. We are never satisfied with anything less than doing the will of God as fully as we know how. When overtaken in a fault we do not give up, we press on to discover how the Spirit can help us with our infirmities. We are pained by human frailties but not paralyzed by them. We press on to more perfect service tomorrow." I have problems remembering. Sometime my mind wanders when I'm reading my Bible and I find myself thinking of something that needs to be done. I have human infirmities!

It was said that Uncle Bud Robinson would have family prayer at night before going to bed. They said that when Uncle Bud started praying for the mail boxes and the public roads they knew he had fallen asleep. How wonderful that the Holy Spirit helpeth us with our infirmities!

The Holy Spirit comforts us for He is the Comforter. He encourages us. He strengthen and helps us. Jesus said in John 14:18, "I will not leave you comfortless (as orphans): I will come to you." In John 16:7 Jesus said to His disciples, "Nevertheless I tell you the truth; It is expedient (best) for you that I go away: for if I go not away, the Comforter will not come unto you, but if I depart, I will send Him unto you." He is closer than the air we breathe. He is the helper. He is the counselor.

F. B. Meyer said, "Think what this means, to have always beside us, not a vague influence, but a Divine person, who waits to be our strength in weakness, our peace in trouble, our wisdom in perplexity, our conqueror in temptation and our counselor in sorrow."

The Holy Spirit only operates in our lives as we allow Him to operate. He is a gentleman. He entreats, draws and appeals but never coerces or forces Himself upon us. We must respond to His tender entreaties by accepting or rejecting. To reject and refuse His tender dealings is to offend the Holy Spirit. Of the three persons of the Godhead He is the most sensitive to slights and insults.

In Isaiah 63:10 we read, "But they (Israel) rebelled and vexed (offended) His Holy Spirit: therefore He was turned to be their enemy and He fought against them." How can we offend the Holy Spirit?

One way to offend the Holy Spirit is to grieve Him. Paul writes in Ephesians 4:30, "Grieve not the Holy Spirit of God, whereby ye are sealed unto the day of redemption." Dr. Dennis Kenlaw said, "The word grieve indicates a tender, intimate, and loving relationship in which someone who loves deeply is hurt." You can grieve a spouse but not a casual acquaintance. You can grieve the Spirit by wrong attitudes such as pride, selfishness, anger, unforgiveness, bitterness or other carnal manifestations. You can grieve the Spirit by saying things that hurt, wound and destroy people and relationships. You can grieve the Spirit by things inconsistent with holy living such as: being careless about your personal prayer life, Bible reading, tithing and church attendance. You can grieve the Spirit by being indifferent to going deeper with God. You are content with being nominal and shallow as a Christian. You can grieve the Spirit by disregard for His guidance and reproofs. The Spirit always checks us if we grieve Him. We must then be obedient and correct the matter or we will further grieve the Holy Spirit. If we continue to grieve the Spirit there comes a point where we will grieve Him from our hearts.

Another way to offend the Holy Spirit is to quench the Spirit. The Apostle Paul wrote in I Thessalonians 5:19, "Quench not the Spirit." Fire is symbolic of the Holy Spirit. To quench is to put out like you put out a fire by throwing water on it. A fire is kindled in our hearts when we get saved. There is a burning desire to know more about Jesus, to please Him, to serve Him and to tell others about Him. Don't quench the Spirit by failing to walk in the light, failing to testify and failing to be obedient to His promptings.

It was probably in the sixties when I was teaching in Mt. Carmel Christian High School. We had a student body of one hundred fifty or more. We had chapel every morning to start the school day. This particular morning one of the maintenance men was in charge. He led us in an opening song and prayer. He was ready to read his scripture and give his message. One of the senior girls stood up and with tears said, "I feel that the Lord wants me to testify." As she testified the Holy Spirit settled down on that student body of teens. Students began to get up, step out and line the altar. We had no message that morning. We had an altar service, and many prayed through. It all happened because one girl did not quench the Spirit.

The Holy Spirit can be offended by insulting Him. The Hebrew writer wrote in Hebrews 10:29, "Of how much sorer punishment, suppose ye, shall he be thought worthy, who hath trodden under foot the Son of God, and hath counted the blood of the covenant, wherewith he was sanctified, an unholy thing, and hath done despite (insult) unto the Spirit of grace." Despite means to treat with contempt. It is the attitude of despising, openly showing disrespect or insulting the Holy Spirit.

Suppose you came to Vancleve, Kentucky. You decide to visit me while you're here. You come on my porch and ring my door bell. I do not come to the door. You hear someone talking and decide it is I. Thinking that I'm hard of hearing you ring again and perhaps knock loudly. I still do not come to the door. You look in the window, and you see that it is I. You knock loudly again and call my name, but I still do not answer the door. After doing this repeatedly for some time you feel that I am not interested in seeing you. You leave feeling insulted, and it is doubtful you will be back anytime soon.

Is it any wonder the Holy Spirit does not speak as loudly or as often as He once did to some individuals when He has been insulted time and again.

You can offend the Holy Spirit by resisting Him. Stephen spoke to those who were about to stone him to death and said, "Ye stiffnecked and uncircumcised in heart and ears, ye do always resist the Holy Ghost: as your fathers did, so do ye" (Acts 7:51).

The Holy Spirit can be lied to according to Acts 5:3a,9a. "Peter said, Ananias, why hath Satan filled thine heart to lie to the Holy Ghost ...? Then Peter said to her (Sapphira), how is it that ye have agreed together to tempt the Spirit of the Lord?" They sold a piece of property and pretended to give all to the church but lied and kept a part for themselves. They pretended a piety they did not have, and God instantly judged them, and they died.

The Holy Spirit can be blasphemed. Jesus said in Matthew 12:31, "All manner of sin and blasphemy shall be forgiven unto men: but the blasphemy against the Holy Ghost shall not be forgiven unto men." This speaks of a wilful, personal, final rejection of the Spirit's testimony by word of mouth which expresses the decision of the heart. By persistent rejection they put themselves beyond the reach of God's forgiveness. There are very few that have ever done this, but it is possible.

The Apostle Paul wrote in Galations 5:25b, "Let us walk (keep in step or obey) in the Spirit." If you are unsaved the Holy Spirit is saying, "You need to repent and seek the Lord for the forgiveness of your sins." The question is, will you obey? If you are a backslider, the Holy Spirit is saying, "You need to repent and be reclaimed." If you have gotten too busy, and God has been crowded out of your life the Holy Spirit is saying, "You need to humbly repent and be restored into a right relationship with your God." The question is, will you be obedient? If you have been saved the Holy Spirit is saying, "You need a pure heart. You need to surrender all. You need to die to self. You need to be Spirit filled. You need to be sanctified wholly." The question is, will you be obedient to the voice of the Holy Spirit? If you are saved and sanctified but conscious you have grieved the Spirit at some point, don't cast away your confidence and give up. Do whatever the Holy Spirit is prompting you to do. Say I'm sorry, apologize, ask forgiveness, pray more, read the Word more, witness more, fast more, tithe and humbly obey the Holy Spirit.

How are you responding to the Holy Spirit? Are you offending or obeying?

Four Calls of The Spirit

The Spirit came in childhood, and pleaded, "Let me in".
But, no, the door was bolted by heedlessness and sin.
"Oh, I'm too young," the child said, "My heart is closed today."
Sadly the spirit listened, then turned and went away.

Again He came and pleaded in youth's bright, happy hour.
He called, but found no answer, for, fettered by sin's power,
The youth lay idly dreaming; "Go, Spirit, not today;
Wait till I've tried life's pleasures." Again He went away.

Once more He came in mercy, in manhood's vigorous prime;
He knocked, but found no entrance, the merchant had no time
"No time to plan for heaven, no time to think or pray."
And so, repulsed and saddened, again He turned away.

Yet once again He pleaded, the man was old and ill
He hardly heard the whisper, his heart was seared and chilled.
"Go, leave me; when I want Thee, I'll send for Thee," he cried.
Then, turning on his pillow, without a hope, he died.

Selected

"Today, if ye hear His voice, harden not your heart."

The Beauty of Holiness

"O worship the Lord in the beauty of holiness" (Psalm 96:9).
"Give unto the Lord the glory due unto His name...worship the
Lord in the beauty of holiness" (I Chronicles 16:29). "And
when he (Jehoshaphat) had consulted with the people, he
appointed singers ... that should praise the beauty of holiness"
(II Chronicles 20:21a). "Give unto the Lord, O ye mighty, give
unto the Lord glory and strength. Give unto the Lord the glory
due unto His name; worship the Lord in the beauty of holiness"
(Psalm 29:1,2).

The Old Testament frequently portrayed God's holiness
causing fear and trembling as it did at Mt. Sinai. In these
portions of God's Word it is portrayed as that which is
beautiful, winsome and attractive.

The beauty of holiness is contrasted with the ugliness of sin.
Holiness is truly beautiful when it is exemplified in the lives of
God's holy people. A holy life is attractive and beautiful. It
captivates the admiration of the sinner and causes him to say,
"That is true and genuine religion. It stimulates a hunger in his
heart and causes him to say, "If I ever get religion that's the
kind I want." I felt that way as a boy when I saw the beauty of
holiness displayed and lived out in the life of one of God's dear
saints in my home area.

God wants to save and sanctify us in two definite works of
grace. He then wants us to live holy lives in such a way that it
will be attractive and winsome causing others to want what we
have.

Rev. John L. Brasher was a sophisticated Methodist
preacher when he heard Commissioner Samuel Logan Brengle
of the Salvation Army preach the message of Scriptural
holiness. John Brasher said, "I could argue with his doctrine
but I could not argue with his face". The beauty of holiness
was shining in the face and spirit of Samuel Logan Brengle and
made John Brasher hungry for the blessing of entire
sanctification.

George W. Ridout wrote a book called *"The Beauty of Holiness."* In it he states that nature combines seven colors to produce pure white. Even so there are seven ingredients which blend together to produce the beauty of holiness in the lives of God's people.

The first ingredient is purity. A filthy stream is repulsive. A clean stream is beautiful. A filthy heart is repulsive. A clean heart is beautiful in the eyes of a holy God. Purity means freedom from defilement and corruption. It speaks of freedom from sins committed and freedom from sin inherited. It means we no longer practice wilful, known sin. It means we have pure desires, pure motives and pure intentions. We are free from deceit, pride, jealousy, hate, bitterness and self centered living.

Purity of heart is a definite act of God's grace. Peter testified in Acts 15:8,9 and said, "And God, which knoweth the hearts, bare them witness giving them the Holy Ghost, even as He did unto us; and put no difference between us and them, purifying their hearts by faith."

Washing is external while cleansing is internal. A sore may be washed and appear to be clean. A few days later there is a redness and evidence of infection. The washing had not gone deep enough. A cleansing agent was needed that would kill the infection hidden deep within.

The song writer said, "The cleansing stream I see, I plunge and O it cleanseth me." Another song says, "What can wash away my sins? Nothing but the blood of Jesus. For my pardon this I see. For my cleansing this my plea. Nothing but the blood of Jesus."

Uncle Bud Robinson was raised in the home of a bootlegger in Tennessee. His family moved to Texas. It was there Bud Robinson heard the gospel and got converted. He soon felt the call to preach. He heard Dr. W. B. Godby preach the message of heart holiness and was made hungry for it. He said, "It was the best religion he ever heard a man preach". He said, "I don't think a man could get it and if he got it I don't think he could live it." He began preaching holiness before he experienced it. One Sunday he preached in one service, "Without holiness no man shall see the Lord" (Hebrews 12:14). In the other service he preached, "The very God of peace sanctify you wholly" (I Thessalonians 5:23). He sought the experience at his own altar and didn't get through. On Monday morning he was thinning corn. He testified that the fire was burning in his soul for holiness. He fell down between two corn rows and began to pray. He testified that pride boiled up, and God skimmed it off. He said jealousy and other carnal traits boiled up and God skimmed them off. He said, "Lord, when you get through with Bud there won't be much left. It looks like I'm all going to skimmins." God seemed to say, "What will be left will be clean." Purity of heart and life is beautiful in the eyes of God and in the eyes of man.

A second ingredient that adds beauty to the holy life is harmony. Discord is irritating while harmony is pleasing. I love to hear a quartet, trio or duet sing in beautiful harmony. The carnal mind opposes God and prevents us from being in harmony with God and His people. Holiness restores us to harmony with God and His people.

The disciples were not in harmony before Pentecost. They were quarreling among themselves the night before the crucifixion as to who was the greatest. They went to the upper room to wait for the Promise of the Father. They had a ten day prayer meeting. They got in one accord and, "Suddenly they were all filled with the Holy Ghost." Peter testified that, "Their hearts were purified by faith." Now they had one desire to please Jesus and do His will. Self will was crucified. They now had one purpose and that was to do the Father's will and to be His witnesses in the world. There was no conflict between their will and God's will. There was harmony and oneness with God and one another in the body of Christ. That kind of harmony is beautiful.

A third ingredient that adds beauty to the holy life is humility. Pride repels. Humility draws. Someone said there are four kinds of pride: face pride, place pride, race pride and grace pride. Another has said that pride is a disease that makes everyone sick except the one that has it.

Humility is essential to receiving anything from God. The sinner must humble himself in genuine repentance in order to receive forgiveness of sin.

Jesus told of a Pharisee and a publican. The Pharisee boasted that he prayed, fasted and tithed. He rejoiced that he was not like the despised publican. The publican smote on his breast and said, "God be merciful to me a sinner" (Luke 18:13). Jesus said the publican went home justified rather than the Pharisee. Why? He was willing to humble himself and acknowledge his sinful condition.

David sinned and cried out to God in Psalm 51:4, "Against Thee, Thee only have I sinned, and done this evil in Thy sight." In verse twelve he says, "Restore unto me the joy of Thy salvation." No backslider can be restored without humbly confessing his or her sin.

The believer must humbly acknowledge the need of a pure heart to be entirely sanctified. Mark records the words of Jesus in his gospel chapter eight and verse thirty four where He says, "Whosoever will come after Me let him deny (disown) himself, and take up his cross, and follow Me."

Isaiah saw God in all his holiness. Seraphims cried, "Holy, holy, holy, is the Lord of hosts: the whole earth is full of His glory" (Isaiah 6:3). When he saw God in all of His holiness he also saw himself and humbly cried out in Isaiah 6:5-7, "Woe is me! For I am undone; because I am a man of unclean lips ... for mine eyes have seen the King, the Lord of hosts. Then flew one of the seraphims unto me, having a live coal in his hand, which he had taken with the tongs from off the altar: and he laid it upon my mouth, and said, Lo, this hath touched thy lips; and thine iniquity is taken away, and thy sin purged."

Prayer is answered on the basis of humility. We read in II Chronicles 7:14, "If my people, which are called by My name, shall humble themselves, and pray, and seek my face, and turn from their wicked ways; then will I hear from heaven, and will forgive their sins, and will heal their land."

Humility is essential to growth in grace. Jesus said in Mark 18:4, "Whosoever therefore, shall humble himself as this little child shall be greatest in the kingdom of heaven."

Humility is essential for spiritual success. In James 4:6 and 10 we read, "God resisteth the proud, but giveth grace to the humble. Humble yourselves in the sight of the Lord and He shall lift you up."

Augustine said, "Do you wish to be great? Then begin by being little." The way up is first the way down in deep humility.

The Apostle Paul wrote in Philippians 2:8 about Jesus, the greatest example of humility and said, "And being found in fashion as a man, He humbled Himself, and became obedient unto death, even the death of the cross."

Where there is holiness, there is humility. It more than any other grace imparts beauty to the Christian life.

The fourth ingredient that adds beauty to the holy life is Christlikeness. The likeness of Christ is truly a beautiful thing. People naturally expect Christians to be like Jesus. The Apostle Paul wrote in Phillippians 2:5, "Let this mind (attitude, disposition, spirit) be in you, which was also in Christ Jesus." Much of professed Christianity is disappointing because it seems to fall short of real Christlikeness.

The Apostle John says Christians are to walk as Christ walked. We read in I John 2:6, "He that saith he abideth in Him (Christ) ought himself also so to walk even as He walked." So we ask, how did Christ walk? He walked carefully. He was careful in meeting temptation. We read in Luke 4:4 and 8, "Jesus answered him (Satan) saying, It is written, that man shall not live by bread alone, but by every word of God. And Jesus answered and said unto him (Satan), Get thee behind me,Satan: for it is written, thou shalt worship the Lord thy God, and Him only shalt thou serve." Christ was careful to always please His Father in heaven. He said in John 8:29, "I do always those things that please Him (the Father)." He was careful to spend time in prayer. In Luke 5:15,16 we read. "But so much more went there a fame abroad of Him: and great multitudes came together to hear, and to be healed by Him of their infirmities. And He withdrew Himself into the wilderness, and prayed." Jesus was careful to see the needs of people. Jesus had compassion on a blind man, a leper, a widow and the multitude. "He saw them as sheep without a shepherd." His rule was to always do His Father's will. Jesus said, "Lo, I come to do Thy will, O God" (Hebrews 10:9). To be Christlike is a combination of righteousness, love, teachableness and patient endurance. John says we are to walk as Jesus walked to be Christlike.

Dr. S. A. Keen's daughter said, "My father is the most Christlike man I ever saw." It was said of Alfred Cookman, of early Methodism, that he was so Christlike in his appearance, from long seasons of communion with the Lord and so absorbed with the spirit of Christ that his very appearance as he walked the streets, reminded people of Jesus and they would stop and gaze at him when he was a great distance away. Samuel Logan Brengle visited in a home where the wife and child were present. That evening the husband came home from work, and the child said, "Daddy, Jesus was in our house today." Rev. Harold Davis, long time professor at the Kentucky Mountain Bible College, was one of the most Christlike men I ever knew. He lived in Christ's presence. Christlikeness is beautiful.

A fifth ingredient that beautifies the holy life is consecration. Consecration, dedication, commitment and devotion are beautiful. In the book of Ruth we have a beautiful story of commitment and dedication. Naomi, her husband, and two sons left Bethlehem in Judah and went to Moab because of famine in Judah. Her sons married Moabite girls, Ruth and Orpah. In time her husband and two sons died leaving three widows. Naomi learns that the famine is over in Judah and decides to return to her home land. She tells her daughters-in-law of her decision, and since she has no more sons to offer as husbands, she insists they stay with their people. Orpah kisses her mother in law goodby and returns to her loved ones. "But Ruth clave unto her (Naomi), and Ruth said, entreat me not to leave thee, or to return from following after thee; for whither thou goest, I will go, and where thou lodgest, I will lodge, thy people shall be my people, and thy God, my God; where thou diest, will I die, and there will I be buried." Because of her devotion she came into the line of Christ. The life that is fully devoted, separated and consecrated to God is a beautiful life.

Consecration is to sanctification what repentance is to justification. It is man's part while the work of cleansing and sanctifying is God's part. Consecration is an actual present surrender to God of the whole person and all he or she possesses. We deed the whole property to Him without reservation.

Frances Ridley Havergal wrote, "Take my life and let it be consecrated Lord to Thee. Take my hands, and let them move at the impulse of Thy love. Take my feet, and let them be swift and beautiful for Thee. Take my voice, and let me sing always, only, for my King. Take my lips, and let them be filled with messages for Thee. Take my silver and my gold, not a mite would I withhold. Take my will and make it Thine, it shall be no longer mine. Take my heart, it is thine own! It shall be Thy Royal Throne. Take my love; my God, I pour at Thy feet its treasure store. Take myself, and I will be, ever, only all for Thee."

Anyone that has done anything worthwhile in the name of Christ has born the marks of consecration. It was said of David Braniard that he so completely severed himself from the outside world that its concerns interested him no more. One thought, one aim, one desire, burning as a sacred passion, burned in his soul. He said, "There appeared, to be nothing of any considerable importance to me but holiness of heart and life and the conversion of the heathen to God." He became a missionary at twenty five and died at thirty.

It was said of John Wesley, "He spent his days among the poor and gave almost all income that he received. In his longing to win the masses, he tried to do all the good he could in the wisest and best way so that he could reach as many as possible for Christ. He lived like a soldier on a campaign, with no surplus baggage, ready at a moment's notice to march. Stormy weather, icy or flooded roads, angry mobs, great distance, or weariness could not stop him. In all it is estimated he traveled 226,000 miles (on foot, horseback, and sometimes in a carriage) and preached 46,000 times."

In 1976 a young man enrolled at Kentucky Mountain Bible College with a call to medical missions. He was outstanding academically and spiritually and graduated with highest honors. He did his pre-med work at the university and then it was medical school. Near the end of his residency, fellow classmates were discussing where they would set up their medical practice. He was asked where he would establish his practice. He replied that he was going to Africa as a medical missionary. Why would he do this? The answer is he was sold out in full surrender to Jesus Christ in total consecration. A life fully consecrated to Jesus Christ is beautiful.

Love is yet another ingredient that beautifies the holy life. The love of a mother is a beautiful thing. The love of a man for a woman is a beautiful thing. I met a man whose wife became afflicted with multiple sclerosis shortly after they were married. She was a trained RN but was only able to practice nursing a short time. She realized what was ahead for her and told her husband to divorce her and go on with his life. His answer was no. He said, "It is til death do us part." I visited her in the nursing home. She could only respond with eye contact. She had been there twenty nine years. Her husband was lovingly at her side. How beautiful to see love like that.

It is most beautiful when a person loves God perfectly and entirely. Love motivates every action. People are human and blunder, but when God sees actions motivated by love, he is pleased. For nearly eighteen years my wife and I lived in the boys' dormitory of Mt. Carmel Christian High School as dorm parents. All four of our children were born during those years. When they were small we told them not to bother the flowers on the campus for they were not ours. They belonged to the school. One day our oldest child brought a bouquet of tulips to his mother. My first reaction was to feel he needed a spanking for he had been disobedient. Then I discovered his motive. It was near Mother's Day and he heard a story in Sunday School of a child that wanted to do something nice for momma at Mother's Day. Thus, he wanted to do something nice for his momma. Needless to say, when I discovered his motive he did not get the spanking. God sees our motive, and even if our service is cumbersome and blundersome, He is pleased when He sees that we love Him.

Love watches like a sentinel on duty lest we should do anything to grieve our God. Jesus said in John 14:15 and 23, "If ye love me, keep my commandments. If a man love me, he will keep my words."

Love wearies not but sacrifices and gives freely of resources and strength. The Apostle Paul was constrained by love to take the gospel to the Gentiles. Polycarp was a disciple of John the beloved disciple of our Lord. He was ordered to curse Christ. He replied, "For eighty six years I have served Him, and He has done no wrong to me. How then dare I blaspheme my king who has saved me." He was martyred because he loved Christ and would not deny Him.

In perfect love, love of Jesus will absorb the soul so that love of self, love of fashion, love of dress, love of money and love of things will have no place. When love is made perfect, we love God with all our heart. God does not have to whip us in line. We walk in line, because we love Him. Perfect love adds beauty to a holy life.

Health adds beauty to the sanctified life. Health is beautiful. Pain, sickness and disease are not beautiful. Holiness is the cure for the problem of sin. It is spiritual wholeness and wellness. In regeneration the outward symptoms are dealt with, and sins are forgiven. This is holiness begun. In entire sanctification the inner infectious nature of sin is cleansed. Jesus gets at the root of the sin problem. We are made whole. Spiritual health is restored. Then we can grow in grace and develop a holy character.

Toplady wrote, "Rock of ages, cleft for me, let me hide myself in Thee, Let the water and the blood from Thy wounded side which flowed be of sin the double cure, save from wrath and make me pure."

These seven elements: purity, harmony, humility, Christlikeness, consecration, love and health all blend together to produce the beauty of holiness in our individual lives.

Holiness is the most beautiful doctrine in the Bible. It is the most beautiful experience to be enjoyed and the most beautiful life to be lived. It never brings clouds. Rather, it brings sunshine. It never splits. It always unites.

It was the beauty of holiness in the lives of God's sanctified children that convicted my heart. Their radiant lives, glowing faces, sweet joyful spirit, and triumphant walk with God made me hungry and caused me to desire what they had.

This is the way I want to live. It doesn't happen all at once in a second crisis experience. Much is achieved by a process of growth and development. As we take the right attitude in the difficult places of life, God fashions us more and more into the likeness of Christ.

The story is told of a boy selling apples on a train. A minister was riding that train. He saw the lad's utter failure to sell apples. The preacher met the boy at the end of the coach. He wanted to help the boy sell his apples. They polished every apple until they were all a brilliant red. The preacher bought an apple and went back to his seat eating it. The boy again passed through the coach with another effort to sell apples. Like magic every apple was sold. What made the difference? The people saw an example, and it looked good. They wanted what they saw.

> "Let the beauty of Jesus be seen in me
> All His wonderful passion and purity
> O Thou Spirit Divine, all my nature refine
> Til the beauty of Jesus be seen in me."

A Holy Ghost Outpouring

Acts 4:24-37

In Acts, chapter two, we have the record of the Jerusalem Pentecost. One hundred-twenty people, all believers, experienced heart cleansing and the infilling of the Holy Spirit in a second work of grace. Curious people came to see what was happening. They said that these men were drunk. Peter said, "This is that which was spoken by the prophet Joel" (Acts 2:16). Three thousand people were converted that day.

In Acts, chapter three, Peter and John went to the temple to pray. They were confronted by a lame beggar. Peter said, "Silver and gold have I none; but such as I have give I thee: in the name of Jesus Christ of Nazareth rise up and walk ... and he leaping up stood, and walked, and entered into the temple, walking, and leaping and praising God" (Acts 3:6,7,8). The people ran to see what was going on, and Peter preached the resurrected Christ to them; the one they rejected and crucified. Peter told them that it was by His power that this man could walk. Priests, the captain of the temple and Sadducees laid hands on Peter and John and put them in prison. But, "Many that heard the Word believed, and the number of the men was about five thousand" (Acts 4:4). The next day Peter and John were threatened and released. "And being let go, they went to their own company (a group of sanctified believers in a prayer meeting), and reported all the chief priests and elders had said to them. And when they heard that they lifted up their voice (as one) to God with one accord ... And when they had prayed ... they were all filled with the Holy Ghost" (Acts 4:23,24,31).

After the initial filling with the Holy Ghost in Acts, chapter two, they were here refilled with the Holy Ghost. There is one initial baptism of the Spirit, but there are many reanointings and fresh outpourings of the Holy Spirit.

In this portion of scripture, we notice some of the effects of this fresh outpouring of the Holy Spirit on the early church.

First, we note that it gave a new perspective to their

stewardship. As stewards all they had belonged to God. They were caretakers or managers of His property. It was all His. What they possessed was a loan from God to be used for His glory. They were partners with God in doing His work and dispensing all He entrusted to them at His direction.

As sanctified Christians all is consecrated to God. He is Lord of our bank account, our investments, our real estate, our time, our talents, our family and our all. We are managers, stewards, caretakers and dispensers of what God entrusts to us, as He directs.

So it was with these early Christians. "Neither was there any among them that lacked: for as many as were possessors of lands or houses sold them (from time to time as need arose), and brought the prices of the things that were sold, and laid them down at the apostles' feet: and distribution was made (from time to time) to every man according as he had need" (Acts 4:34,35).

Barnabas, the son of encouragement, sold a piece of property and gave the proceeds to the church. He was not unlike some people that I have known. One man was willing to sell an expensive horse in order to do his part in a church building program. A man and his wife sold a beautiful lake front property and moved into a much smaller house in order to make a large contribution to the building of a new holiness church.

The tithe is the minimum of Christian giving. To give less is to rob God. As a steward over all God entrusts to us He has a right to call for any or all as He chooses.

A fresh outpouring of the Spirit will give a right perspective to our stewardship. We first give ourselves to God in full surrender. If God has all of us He has all we have. He has our time, talents, resources, energy, our all. When the Apostle Paul was encouraging the Corinthian Christians to participate in the offering for the poor, suffering, persecuted Christians in the mother church in Jerusalem, he cited the example of the Philippian Christians. He said, "They first gave their own selves to the Lord, and unto us by the will of God" (II Corinthians 8:5b).

The fresh outpouring of the Spirit on the early church gave a new authority to the Scriptures. "They spake the Word with boldness (assurance, confidence, power, plainness, frankness, and authority)" (Acts 4:31b).

The Holy Spirit inspired the Word of God, the Bible. "For the prophecy came not in old time by the will of man: but holy men of God spake as they were moved (carried along, borne along, or influenced) by the Holy Ghost" (II Peter 1:21). Men spoke from God. God told them what to say, and they said it, and they wrote it.

The Holy Spirit reveals the Word. Paul wrote in I Corinthians 2:9-11, "But as it is written, eye hath not seen nor ear heard, neither have entered into the heart of man, the things which God hath prepared for them that love Him but God hath revealed them unto us by His Spirit: for the Spirit searcheth all things, yea, the deep things of God, for what man knoweth the things of a man, save the spirit of man which is in him? Even so the things of God knoweth no man, but the Spirit of God." I do not know your plans, purposes or intentions, but your spirit does for it dwells in your body. Even so the Holy Spirit dwells in God and knows God's thoughts, plans and purposes and is able to reveal them unto us.

The Holy Spirit teaches, instructs and illuminates the Word. Paul wrote in I Corinthians 2:12,13, "Now we have received not the spirit of the world, but the spirit which is of God; that we might know the things that are freely given to us of God. Which things also we speak, not in the words which man's wisdom teacheth, but which the Holy Ghost teacheth; comparing spiritual things with spiritual."

"The natural (unregenerated) man receiveth not the things of the Spirit of God: for they are foolishness unto him: neither can he know them, because they are spiritually discerned. But he that is spiritual (born of the Spirit or filled with the Spirit) judgeth (discerneth) all things (by the aid of the Holy Spirit)" (I Corinthians 2;14,15a).

The Holy Spirit gives a right interpretation of Scripture. He is the conserver of orthodoxy. He guides into all truth. A fresh outpouring of the Holy Spirit gives power to the written Word as well as power to the preached word.. Every preacher needs a fresh anointing of the Holy Spirit in order to preach with power and authority.

A fresh outpouring of the Holy Spirit gave the early church a new consciousness of sin. Peter preached in the power of the Spirit on the day of Pentecost as recorded in Acts 2:22,23, and 36. He said, "Ye men of Israel, hear these words; Jesus of Nazareth, a man approved of God among you by miracles and wonders and signs, which God did by Him in the midst of you, as ye yourselves also know: Him, being delivered by the determinate counsel and foreknowledge of God, ye have taken, and by wicked hands have crucified and slain. Therefore let all the house of Israel know assuredly, that God hath made that same Jesus, whom ye have crucified, both Lord and Christ." Conviction immediately gripped the hearts of the people. Acts 2:37 tells us, "They were pricked (cut) in their heart, and said ... what shall we do?" Peter answered in verse thirty eight and said, "Repent!" Jesus said, "When He (the Holy Spirit) is come, He will reprove (convict and convince) the world of sin, and of righteousness and of judgment" (John 16:8).

The Holy Spirit makes sin appear as sin. Carnal reasoning causes us to excuse, conceal and compromise with sin. The Holy Spirit uncovers and reveals sin for what it is. The Holy Spirit never points out sin where it isn't. It may be an act or acts of sin for which one needs to repent. It may be the polluted nature of sin for which we need cleansing. Someone said, "The weakness of Christians is often a greater problem than the wickedness of the world." It was a recognition of this condition that showed Hannah Whithall Smith her need of heart holiness. In her book, The Christian's Secret of a Happy Life, she described her condition. She said, "I was converted in my 26th year. But my heart was ill at ease. I did not grow in grace, and at the end of eight years of my Christian life I was forced to make the sorrowful admission that I had not even as much power over sin as when I was first converted. In the presence of temptation I found myself weakness itself. It was not my outward walk that caused me sorrow, though I can see now that it was far from what it ought to have been; but it was sins of my heart that troubled me - coldness, deadness, want of Christian love, roots of bitterness, want of a meek and quiet spirit. Sin still had more or less dominion over me, and I did not come up to the Bible standard."

A fresh outpouring of the Holy Spirit will give a new consciousness of sin. Sins need to be forgiven. The sin nature needs to be cleansed in a second work of grace called entire sanctification.

A fresh outpouring of the Spirit gave the early church a new passion for souls. Acts 4:33 says the apostles gave witness.

Why did they witness? They saw sinners lost and doomed for the torments of hell. Sinners are often blinded by materialism. They are blind to the joys of salvation and the peace that Christ alone can give. They are blind to the glories of heaven and the awfulness of coming judgment. They are blind to the torments of hell and the length of eternity.

Sinners are asleep. They have been drugged by the opium of sin. They are dead to the things of the Spirit and to fellowship with Christ and His church.

While they saw sinners as lost, they saw themselves as responsible. They felt the great need of praying for the lost and of telling them of Christ's love for them. They wanted to tell of Christ's power to save, to deliver from sin's bondage and to transform their lives.

They realized they were once just like them. They were once lost, blind, bound and dead in trespasses and sin. But God in His mercy allowed the light of the Gospel to open their blinded eyes. They were freed from the bondage and slavery of sin. It was not because they deserved it. It was because of God's great love and mercy. But God loves other lost sinners just as He loved them.

They had been to Pentecost. They had just experienced a fresh outpouring of the Holy Spirit. Their hearts were set on fire with holy love to witness and win the lost.

While a student in Asbury College in 1958, God visited the campus with a fresh outpouring of His Spirit. The immediate result was that young people got on the phone and witnessed to family and friends. They went to churches, street meetings and jails, witnessing and seeking the lost.

We need a fresh outpouring of the Holy Spirit in order to have a proper passion for the lost.

A fresh outpouring of the Holy Spirit gave the early church a new love for the saints. Acts 4:32 says they had one heart and one soul. They loved one another. They had unity and harmony. They cared for one another. "They had all things common" (Acts 4:32b). If one person had a need, the rest sacrificed to meet the need of their brother or sister in the Lord. They minimized human weaknesses, faults and differences. They did not gossip and criticize one another. They loved one another, and that was the mark of the early church.

We need a fresh outpouring of the Holy Spirit in order to have a proper love and appreciation of our brothers and sisters in Christ. It will cause us to reconcile differences. It will cause us to apologize for unkind words. It will further cause us to be loving in what we say to and about our brother or sister in Christ.

This fresh outpouring of the Holy Spirit gave the early church a new power to stand. They prayed in verse twenty-nine, "Lord, behold their threatenings; and grant unto Thy servants, that with all boldness they may speak Thy Word." They wanted boldness to witness. They wanted boldness to not compromise truth and to be able to bear persecution.

Persecution is raging in the world today in more than sixty countries. Christians face torture, slavery, beatings, wrongful imprisonment and death because they follow Jesus Christ.

The church needs a fresh outpouring of God's Spirit today in order that we might take our stand for Christ in the midst of a hostile world, regardless of the cost.

The fresh outpouring of the Holy Spirit gave the early Christians a new urgency to serve. They realized the shortness of time and the soon return of Christ. They remembered the ascension of their Lord from the Mount of Olives. There Jesus gave His disciples final instruction. Suddenly, gravity lost its hold, and Jesus ascended. The clouds received Him out of their sight. Two men in white stood with them and said, "Ye men of

Galilee, why stand ye gazing up into heaven? This same Jesus, which is taken up from you into heaven, shall so come in like manner as ye have seen Him go into heaven" (Acts 1:11).

They saw the fields white to harvest and went immediately to the task. Three thousand were converted at one time. Five thousand were converted at another time. Daily people were being added to the church.

We need a fresh outpouring of the Holy Spirit to give us an urgency to serve and win the lost of our day.

I thank God for every outpouring of the Holy Spirit I have been privileged to witness. When I was a boy of eight years of age God visited our home church in Melbourne, Kentucky, with a powerful revival and outpouring of the Holy Spirit. It was in that revival that I first was converted. As a student at Mt. Carmel Christian High School and Kentucky Mountain Bible College I witnessed the outpouring of the Holy Spirit. At Asbury College in 1958, the Holy Spirit was outpoured in a spontaneous revival where many were saved, reclaimed, sanctified and blessed.

In the early 1990's the Kentucky Mountain Bible College was seeking accreditation with (AABC) The Accrediting Association of Bible Colleges. An examining team was on campus for the final step before accreditation was granted. We were seated at the dinner table at the Bible College. Board members, administrators and the examining team were all present. Conversation was turned to the outpouring of the Holy Spirit that I was privileged to witness while a student at Asbury College. After relating my experience during that revival, a member of the examining committee commented that he and his wife were converted in such a meeting. He went on to say that his children had never witnessed such an outpouring of the Holy Spirit.

Can we know a fresh outpouring of God's Holy Spirit today? I believe we can. The question is how? How did it happen in Acts 4? The answer is in Acts 4:31 which says, "When they had prayed the place was shaken ... and they were all filled with the Holy Ghost."

Prayer is the key to every genuine revival and outpouring of the Holy Spirit. If we would see a fresh outpouring of the Holy Spirit we must get desperate in prayer and obedience.

The chorus says:

"I'll say yes, Lord, yes; to your will and to your way.
I'll say yes, Lord, yes; I will trust you and obey.
When your Spirit speaks to me, with my whole heart
I'll agree and my answer will be, yes, Lord, yes!"

Life's Greatest Achievement

Colossians 2:6,7
Ephesians 5:1-18
"And Enoch walked with God, and he was not; for God took him ... before his translation he had this testimony that he pleased God" (Genesis 5:24 and Hebrews 11:5b).

If I were to take a poll and ask what each person considered to be life's greatest achievement, I'm certain I would get a variety of differing answers. Some, no doubt, would feel it would be to get money and the things money can get such as real estate, stocks and bonds. Others might feel that their greatest achievement would be success in politics, business, the military, theatrics or athletics.

I was impressed some years ago when I learned that Bobby Richardson was quitting major league baseball. He had been star second baseman for the New York Yankees. He had been all star second baseman for the American League. At the age of thirty and making good money he quit. Many were critical of his quitting in what was considered his prime with the possibility of more money, and additional fame. He answered his critics and said, "My outlook on life and baseball is expressed in the words of Walt Hundley's poem, "God's Hall of Fame." Hundley said, "I tell you friend, I wouldn't trade my name, however small, that's written there beyond the stars in that Celestial Hall, for all the famous names on earth, or glory that they share. I'd rather be an unknown down here and have my name up there."

As a boy I dreamed dreams as to what would be the greatest achievement of my life. A professional athlete seemed to top the list. I'm certain I would have never attained it had I pursued it. But, on March 8, 1952, the Lord reclaimed me and forgave all my sins. On March 9, 1952, He sanctified me wholly. Since those two crises experiences God has changed my set of values. I have long since come to realize that the greatest achievement of a life time is not to get fortune and fame or have your name on the headlines of the sports page in the newspaper. I feel with all my heart that the greatest achievement of a life time is to walk with God and please Him. This has become my one consuming desire and ambition.

It was not popular to walk with God in Enoch's day nor has it ever been. Genesis chapter five is a genealogy telling how different Bible characters lived, had families and died. Enoch is an exception. He did more than live, have a family and die. Enoch walked with God and did such a good job of it that God took him to heaven, and he didn't have to go by way of the grave.

We are not told how Enoch walked, but the Bible is clear on how we should walk if we would attain a like achievement with Enoch. The Apostle Paul gives us five pieces of instruction.

First, Paul tells us to walk as we received Him (Colossians 2:6,7). This presupposes a time and a place where we received Christ as our personal savior. We repented and trusted Christ for the forgiveness of our sins. We were born again. Paul said that we keep saved the same way we got saved. So we ask, "What was necessary to find salvation if that is what is necessary to retain salvation?"

Perhaps the first thing necessary to find salvation is humility. We must first humbly acknowledge and confess our sins in order to experience forgiveness of sin. There must be humility before we can receive anything from God. In James 4:6b and 10 we read, "God resisteth the proud but giveth grace to the humble. Humble yourselves in the sight of the Lord, and He shall lift you up."

In Luke 18 Jesus told us about a publican and a Pharisee. The Pharisee boasted and said, "I pray, I fast, I tithe and I'm glad I'm not like this despised publican." The publican smote on his breast and prayed, "God be merciful to me a sinner." Jesus said the publican went home justified rather than the Pharisee. Why? He was willing to humble himself and confess his sin. Paul said that we keep saved the same way we got saved. The same humility required to find salvation is necessary to retain it. "As ye have therefore received Christ Jesus the Lord, so walk ye in Him" (Colossians 2:6).

When I got saved, I made some vows to the Lord. I promised the Lord I would make my wrongs right, I'd live for Him, I'd serve Him and do anything He wanted me to do. If I'm going to walk with the Lord I must maintain my vows. "As ye received Christ Jesus the Lord so walk ye in Him."

It took a real purpose to become a Christian. If loved ones or best friends are not Christians we must purpose that we are going to be a Christian. We often sing, "I have decided to follow Jesus, no turning back, no turning back." The same purpose it took to become a Christian is required to remain a Christian. "As ye have therefore received Christ Jesus the Lord, so walk ye in Him" (Colossians 2:6).

The final step in becoming a Christian is a step of faith. We are justified by faith. We are sanctified by faith, and we walk by faith. We cannot depend on our feelings. The evangelist, C. W. Ruth, once said, "I feel just as good when I don't feel good as I do when I do feel good because I don't go by feeling anyhow." Our walk with Christ is a walk of faith. "As ye have therefore received Christ Jesus the Lord, so walk ye in Him" (Colossians 2:6).

I'm talking about Life's Greatest Achievement which is walking with God and pleasing Him. Paul told us we must walk as we received Him.

Paul's second piece of instruction is "Walk in love" (Ephesians 5:2). We are to walk in love because of Christ's love. He first loved us, and love begets love. Love is reciprocal. If you were drowning and someone risked his life and rescued you, I'm sure you would love and appreciate him for what he had done. God sent His Son on the greatest rescue mission this world has ever known. He came to rescue us from sin and destruction. We ought to love Him. The song says, "I was sinking deep in sin; ... but ... love lifted me." Another song says, "In loving kindness Jesus came, My soul in mercy to reclaim, And from the depths of sin and shame Thro' grace He lifted me. From sinking sand He lifted me; With tender hand He lifted me. From shades of night to planes of light, Oh, praise His name, He lifted me!"

Love sacrifices and serves without thought of reward. Why will a mother walk the floor through the long hours of the night and forfeit her sleep to care for the feverish child in her arms? She doesn't call it sacrifice. She does it because of a mother's love for her child. Love will send us to the ends of the earth. It will cause us to leave family and friends and risk our all because we love Jesus.

If we could call the Apostle Paul to the witness stand and say, "Paul, why did you do what you did? You were well educated. You could have settled down in your home town of Tarsus and been a great educator. You could have made a lot of money and a great name for yourself. Instead, you went around the world of your day making tents. You suffered many perils.

You were shipwrecked, imprisoned, stoned and left for dead, and finally you were executed for your faith in Christ." I think Paul would say something like this. "One day I was on the road to Damascus to arrest Christians. A great light from heaven smote me to the ground. My physical sight was temporarily taken from me, but my spiritual eyes were opened. I saw Jesus. I saw where the thorns pierced His brow. I saw the nail wounds in His hands and feet and where the spear was thrust into His side. I saw God's great love for me by giving His Son to die for my sins. That day the love of God was shed abroad in my heart by the Holy Ghost. A few days later on Straight Street in the city of Damascus I met godly, saintly Ananias. That day I was filled with the Holy Ghost, and my heart was made perfect in love. Since then the love of Christ has constrained me to take the gospel to the whole world." When we love Jesus with a heart of perfect love, no sacrifice is to great and no service too demanding.

Love is true and faithful. The wife that loves her husband does not flirt with other men. The husband that loves his wife does not flirt with other women. If we love Jesus we will not flirt with the world. John said in I John 2:15b, "If any man love the world the love of the Father is not in him." James said in James 4:4b, "Know ye not that friendship of the world is enmity with God?" Love for Jesus rules out carelessness and unfaithfulness. It will cause us to be faithful to the church, to prayer, to Bible reading, to tithing, to witnessing and to answering God's call to service. It will cause us to be faithful to our Lord and Savior, Jesus Christ. He will be first on our priority list.

Love is considerate of others. The Apostle Paul wrote in I Corinthians 13:4,5 according to the Amplified New Testament, "Love endures long and is patient and kind, love never is envious nor boils over with jealousy; is not boastful or vainglorious, does not display itself haughtily. It is not conceited, arrogant, and inflated with pride; it is not rude (unmannerly), and does not act unbecomingly. Love does not insist on its own rights or its own way, for it is not self seeking. It is not touchy or fretful or resentful."

In the new birth God's love is shed abroad in our hearts by the Holy Ghost (Romans 5:5). In entire sanctification our love is made perfect. It is no longer mixed with self love. Jesus said in John 14:15 and 23a, "If ye love Me, keep my commandments. If a man love me, he will keep My words." His commandments are not grievous, galling or irksome. They are a delight, because we love the lawgiver. His law is in our hearts.

We're talking about life's greatest achievement - walking with God and pleasing Him. Paul says, "Walk in love."

The third piece of instruction is found in Ephesians 5:1 where the Apostle says, "Walk as dear children." Children are interesting. We have been blessed to have four children, and they are all precious and different. Children are imitators. Dad gets hammer and nails to do a repair job. Son wants to do as dad does even if he hits the wrong nail. Wife mixes up a cake. Daughter wants to do the same even if it is a mud cake. John says in I John 2:6, "He that saith he abideth in Him ought himself also so to walk, even as He walked." John says that children of God ought to imitate their heavenly Father. We are to walk as He walked. How did Christ walk? He walked free from sin. In I John 3:9 we read, "Whosoever is born of God doth not commit sin; for His seed remaineth in him: and he cannot sin, because he is born of God." John says we cannot be a born again Christian and be sinning at the same time anymore than one can be drunk and be sober at the same time. John says, "He that committeth sin is of the devil" (I John 3:8a). In I John 2:1 John says, "My little children, these things write I unto you, that ye sin not. And if any man sin, we have an advocate with the Father, Jesus Christ the righteous." John recognizes that it is possible not to sin. He also recognizes that it is possible to be tripped up by the enemy of our soul and to fall into sin. He tells us that if that happens we should not give up and say, "I can't live the Christian life." He tells us that we have an advocate or an attorney, at the right hand of the Father, Jesus Christ, our elder brother. John says to run to Jesus, confess the sin immediately, and get it under the blood. You don't have to wait for the next revival or altar service. This is not a provision for a sinning religion. It is an emergency provision for someone that loves God and has been overtaken in a moment of temptation and falls into a sin. Christ wants to save us from sin, cleanse us from the sin nature and empower us by His Holy Spirit to live in victory over sin. Christ walked free from sin and wants us to do the same.

Christ walked with compassion on the blind man, the leper, the widow and the multitude. He saw the multitude as sheep without a shepherd. He wants us to walk with the same compassion that he had on the lost, the hurting and the needy that are all around us.

Christ was careful to always do the will of His Father in heaven. He wants us to walk as He walked with the same carefulness to always please our heavenly Father. We are to walk as dear children and imitate Christ.

Another thing we observe about a child is the child's obedience. Some children whine and fuss. They don't want to obey. Others, though they may be rare, obey quickly and gladly without argument. I'm sure that's the kind of obedience God wants from His dear children.

Another thing we note in a child is the child's trust. We have four children. They all grew up in the rural area of Eastern Kentucky. If, when they were small, I would have taken them to Cincinnati, Ohio, when traffic was at its peak and told them to go down the street to a certain location and promised to meet them in a half hour, they would have been scared to death. But, if I would have said, "Take Daddy's hand, and let's go." They would have gone unafraid. What made the difference? They had hold of Daddy's hand and trusted Daddy to take care of them. If we can put that kind of trust in an earthly father, how much more should we trust our heavenly Father. We are to walk as dear children.

Yet, another thing that stands out is the reverence of a child for his father. I had a wonderful father. He was a mechanic, and I thought he was the very best. If one of my buddies would say anything to the contrary, I was ready to set him straight. I revered the name of my father. How much more should we revere the name of our heavenly Father. It hurts deeply to hear anyone blaspheme or speak irreverently of my heavenly Father and His Son, my Lord and Savior Jesus Christ. We ought not only reverence His name, we ought to reverence His day. It is not a day for buying and selling or pleasure seeking. It is a holy day set aside for worship of almighty God. We ought to reverence His house which is sanctified and set apart for the holy purpose of worship. We are to walk as dear children.

If we would achieve life's greatest achievement of walking with God and pleasing Him, Paul says we are to walk as we received Him. We are to walk in love. We are to walk as dear children. Fourth, Paul says we are to walk circumspectly (Ephesians 5:15). This word, circumspectly, means we are to walk cautiously, on guard, prudently and watchfully. We have an adversary and are admonished to beware the wiles or trickery of the devil.

The word, circumspectly, further means to walk correctly, accurately, consistently and conscientiously. It has been said that Christians are the only Bible many sinners read. Someone else said, "What we do speaks so loud folk can't hear what we say." If we profess to be Christians, we should live like it, dress like it, and act like it in all our actions, reactions and transactions.

The word, circumspectly, finally means to apply all our effort. We are not to be lazy or to play church. We are to put our all into serving Jesus Christ. We are to redeem the time. We are to buy up the time and not waste it, because the days are evil. Adam Clark said that means, "The days are dangerous, full of trouble and temptation. Only the watchful will keep their garments clean and be ready for Christ's return." We are to walk circumspectly.

A final piece of instruction is given in Ephesians 5:18. Paul says, "We are to walk filled with the Spirit." We are to walk sanctified wholly. If not, a carnal root of bitterness may spring up and trouble you, thus causing you not to walk pleasing to your Lord. To be sanctified wholly one must first be emptied of all sin and self. Sanctification is an act of cleansing and followed by the infilling of the Holy Ghost. However, God will do neither the cleansing nor the filling until you yield in total surrender to the whole will of God.

"Be filled with the Spirit" is a command. It is absolutely necessary to walk with God and please Him. Paul is saying that we are to be continually filled with the Spirit. We are to get filled, and then, keep filled. There is one initial filling, but there are many refillings or fresh outpourings of the Holy Spirit. Spirit fullness is absolutely necessary for victorious living and fruitful service.

The Apostle Paul has given us five pieces of instruction on how to achieve life's greatest achievement of walking with God and pleasing Him. He said we are to walk as we received Him; we are to walk in love; we are to walk as dear children; we are to walk circumspectly, and we are to walk filled with the Spirit.

Enoch walked with God and pleased Him without all this instruction that Paul has given us. Thus, with the Word of God, the help of the Holy Spirit, and the help of God's people, we ought to be able to walk with God and please Him in our day.

Someone said that Enoch was walking with God and enjoying the fellowship so much that he lost consciousness of time. Finally he realized that the sun was dying in the west, and he was a long ways from home. He said, "Father, I must hurry home. The family needs me." God seemed to say, "Enoch, it´s closer to my house than it is to yours. You come on home with me." God took him home with Him. There is no night there. It is one unending day. Enoch has forever been with the Lord.

Are you walking with God? Is God pleased? If there is any

unforgiven sin in your life, God is not pleased. You need to repent and be forgiven. If there are any remains of the carnal self life, God is not pleased. You need cleansing and the sanctifying grace of God in a second work of God's amazing grace. What are you trying to achieve with your life?

Dr. Lela G. McConnell, the founder of the Kentucky Mountain Holiness Association, went to heaven April 7, 1970. I with others were privileged to be at her bedside and hear her final words. She testified, "I have no pain, no burden, no fear. My end has come and my soul is full of glory." She achieved life's greatest achievement. She walked with God and had the testimony that God was pleased.

Dr. Dennis Kinlaw said, "The highest divine compliment is the privilege of walking with God." A person can have all the success of this world, but if he fails to walk with God and please Him he's a failure for all eternity.

Holiness and Heaven

Psalm 93

"Holiness becometh thine house, O Lord, forever" (Psalm 93:5b).

The highway of holiness was laid by the blood of Christ from the closed gates of the Garden of Eden to the open portals of glory. It reaches from Eden's paradise lost to heaven's paradise regained. Isaiah saw this and declared, "A highway shall be there, and a way, and it shall be called the way of holiness, the unclean shall not pass over it" (Isaiah 35:8b). All who reach the heavenly city must travel this holy highway.

There are five things about holiness and heaven to which I wish to direct your attention.

First, heaven will be pure. John the Revelator declared, "And there shall in no wise enter into it (heaven) any thing that defileth, neither whatsoever worketh abomination, or maketh a lie; but they which are written in the Lamb's book of life" (Revelation 21:27).

Holiness is the eternal plan of God. Paul writes in Ephesians 1:4 and says, "According as He (God) hath chosen us in Him (Christ) before the foundation of the world, that we should be holy and without blame before Him in love." The picture I see is God sitting at the eternal drawing board drawing up a blueprint for this old world. When He came to the subject of man, He specified that "Man should be holy." God has never scrapped the blueprint. It is still in effect. He means for man to be holy.

There are at least two reasons for such a plan. First, God specified that man should be holy in order that he might fellowship with a holy God. When God made man in the beginning, He made him in His own likeness, pure and holy. Man enjoyed wonderful fellowship with his Maker as they walked and talked together in the cool of the day, which possibly suggests morning and evening. However, something happened that marred that fellowship, and man was separated from that beautiful paradise. That something was sin. Sin always separates from God. The only way for that fellowship to be regained was for God to send His Son to an old rugged cross and die. There He made an atonement sufficient to bridge the gap between sinful man and a Holy God. Thus, man can be redeemed and once again have an intimate relationship with our Holy God.

A second reason why God planned for man to be holy is that God was planning for our happiness. Holiness and happiness are like siamese twins. They go together and are inseparable. We don't seek happiness. We seek holiness, and happiness comes as a by-product. God is not a hi-jacker. He does not take the good from us and give us the refuse or culls. He has from all eternity been looking out for our best interests. Sin brings heartache, heartbreak and ruin. Holiness brings happiness. I can assure you, on the authority of God's Word, that if you line up with God's plan and get truly saved and sanctified wholly, you can have a happy life, a happy home and a happy eternity.

Holiness is the central theme of the Bible. From Genesis to Revelation holiness is paramount. William Deal said, "Sinai is holiness demanded, Calvary is holiness supplied, Pentecost is holiness executed, a sanctified saint is holiness demonstrated, and heaven will be holiness consummated forever and ever." The great central concern of Bible prophecy, Bible poetry, every precept, promise and prayer in Scripture is to bring man to holiness. God insists on having a holy people.

Holiness is the very essence of God. God is holy. Peter wrote, "But as He which hath called you is holy, so be ye holy in all manner conversation (behavior, conduct, life style); because it is written, be ye holy; for I am holy" (I Peter 1:15,16). Heaven is God's home or dwelling place. Holiness is becoming and fitting to where God lives. If you went to God's house, you would not expect to find beer in the refrigerator, ash trays scattered about, a deck of cards on the table, wicked magazines and lewd pictures glaring at you. These things are not becoming in God's house. If these things are not becoming in God's house, then what about the houses of God's people? The poet, Lois Kendall Blanchard, wrote,

"If Jesus Came To Your House"

If Jesus came to your house to spend a day or two -
   If He came unexpectedly, I wonder what you'd do.
Oh, I know you'd give your nicest room to such an honored guest,
   And all the food you'd serve to Him would be the very best,
And you would keep assuring Him you're glad to have Him there -
   That serving Him in your own home is joy beyond compare.

But when you saw Him coming, would you meet Him at the door
   With arms outstretched in welcome to your heavenly visitor?
Or would you have to change your clothes before you let Him in?
   Or hide some magazines and put the Bible where they'd been?
Would you turn off the radio (and TV) and hope He hadn't heard?
   And wish you hadn't uttered that last, loud, hasty word?

Would you hide your worldly music and put some hymn books out?
   Could you let Jesus walk right in, or would you rush about?
And I wonder - if the Savior spent a day or two with you,
   Would you go right on doing the things you always do?
Would you go right on saying the things you always say?
   Would life for you continue as it does from day to day?

Would your family conversation keep up its usual pace?
   And would you find it hard each meal to say a table grace?
Would you sing the songs you always sing, and read the books you read?
   And let Him know the things on which your mind and spirit feed?
Would you take Jesus with you everywhere you'd planned to go?
   Or would you, maybe, change your plans for just a day or so?

Would you be glad to have Him meet your very closest friends?

Or would you hope they'd stay away until His visit ends? Would you be glad to have Him stay forever on and on?

Or would you sigh with great relief when He at last was gone?

It might be interesting to know the things that you would do

If Jesus Christ in person came to spend some time with you.

A sinning religion may get a person through a crooked, sinful world and a cold, dead church, but it will never get you into a holy heaven. Heaven will be pure.

Secondly, Heaven will be prepared. Jesus said, "I go to prepare a place for you" (John 14:2b). Heaven will be complete. Nothing will be lacking in its furnishings, beauty, grandeur and glory.

Ancient history reveals that the city of Corinth, when in the height of its glory, was one of the most beautiful cities of the world. Its lovely statuary, magnificent columns of Corinthian architecture, and its illustrious natural scenery have never been surpassed. I was privileged to visit Corinth in 1968. Even in ruins it was indeed a beautiful place with the AcroCorinth jutting 1800 feet into the heavens in the background. The blue water of the Ionian Sea was in the foreground. Yet to people living in these gorgeous surroundings the Apostle Paul said, "Eye hath not seen, nor ear heard, neither have entered into the heart of man, the things God hath prepared for them that love Him" (I Corinthians 2:9). The real meaning is that no human eye nor mind could conceive the great plan of redemption. God alone conceived it and revealed it to us by His Spirit. But certainly no human mind can conceive the glories He has prepared for His redeemed children in heaven.

My father went home to heaven in 1963. For thirteen years after Dad's passing, Mother lived alone in Alexandria, Kentucky. I have one sister, and she lived an hour away from Mother on the north side of Cincinnati, Ohio. I lived three hours away in Eastern Kentucky. I kept in close contact with

Mother and went to see her at every opportunity. On occasion I would be preaching in revival in Indiana, Michigan or Ohio. I would call Mother and tell her that the meeting would be closing on a certain Sunday night. I would often be keyed up after a meeting and would just as soon get in my car and drive. I would inform Mother that I would leave after the final service and drive to her house. I would arrive at midnight or later. When I pulled my car in the driveway, the lights would come on at the corners of the house. The garage door would open. I had no electronic device to trigger those things. It was Mother. There she stood in the doorway of the garage. I would pull the car into the garage and get out and express my love to my mother. We would go into the house. Mother would ask me if I would like a piece of pie. Mother knew the kind I liked for I liked only two kinds, hot and cold. Mother did the things mothers do when the children come home. She made special preparation.

God's great family is coming home. They're coming from the east, the west, the north and the south. Jesus has gone to prepare for the great homecoming when all God's great family is gathered home.

Thirdly, Heaven will be a place. Jesus said, "I go to prepare a place for you" (John 14:2b). Heaven is the capitol of the celestial universe just as Washington, D.C. is the capitol of the United States of America. It is the home of the bride of Christ, the church, the redeemed and blood-washed of all the ages. It is a foursquare city, which guarantees an abundance of room for all God's redeemed children.

William Deal said, "The boundary would reach from Maine to Florida and from the Atlantic coast to Denver, Colorado. It would cover all of Britain, Ireland, France, Spain, Italy, Germany, Australia, European Turkey, and European Russia taken together."

Babylon was the largest city of the ancient world being sixty miles in circumference. This city is over one hundred times as large, being six thousand miles in circumference.

Think of a city with no less than eight million streets a mile apart in each direction and one fifth the diameter of the earth in length. Think of each individual having a personal mansion with one hundred rooms furnished with such resplendent glories that angels can hardly describe it. Think of angels as servants. Think of being entertained by the beautiful music of heaven. Think of the continual surprises as God the Father and Jesus Christ, the Son, show us their limitless and inexhaustible resources. It may take a million millenniums to get acquainted with our heavenly inheritance.

You say, "Brother Neihof, you're getting reckless with your imagination." Perhaps I am. When I was a boy growing up in Northern Kentucky I lived in the country. My father lost interest in the farm and went into auto mechanics. He started his business across the road from where we lived. When I was about two years of age, he moved his business to the little village of Melbourne, Kentucky. This was about three and one-half miles from our house. The old building that my father first used in his mechanical business still stood across the road from our house. Dad had stored there a 1927 Chevrolet truck that had been his first tow truck in his mechanical business. I used to love to go across the road and climb up in the cab of that old truck and pretend like I was driving. In my imagination I was seeing people and going many places. But, friends, heaven is not an imaginary, make believe place. Heaven is not a fairy tale or a fantasy land. Heaven is a real place, and by the grace of God I intend to go there. I want to see you there.

Fourthly, heaven will be perfect. John wrote in Revelation 21:4, "God shall wipe away all tears from their eyes; and there shall be no more death, neither sorrow, nor crying, neither shall there be any more pain: for the former things are passed away." There will be no crippled, deformed or retarded people in heaven. They will be perfectly healed.

I saw a boy that had no arms. He had only a stub of an arm sticking straight out from his body on either side. A hand was attached to each stub. He was trying to play with a group of children who where normally formed. My heart went out to that child. Thank God for the hope of heaven where no one in that condition will be seen, for heaven will bring perfect healing.

There will be no one in heaven suffering from arthritis or any other disease or affliction. In 1953, I graduated from Mt. Carmel Christian High School. The summer following graduation I sang in a male school quartet and traveled with Dr. Lela G. McConnell, the founder and then president of the Kentucky Mountain Holiness Association. We traveled to the east coast and daily had services in churches and camp meetings. We had a service in northeast Ohio. The following morning we had prayer with our hostess before leaving. She asked us to go down the street a short distance and sing for a lady bedfast with crippling arthritis. We went into the living room of the home where the dear woman was lying on a cot. It was a hot summer day, and we could see that under the sheet that covered her was a twisted and gnarled body. She only moved as others moved her. She had been in this condition for five years. When we looked into her face, we saw the glory of another world. Thank God for the hope of heaven where there will never be a scene like that for heaven will be perfect.

There will be no death in heaven. Our neighbor had preached on Sunday. While in the pulpit preaching he had an aneurysm in the back of his head. He was rushed to the hospital but died the same day. He left a wife and three small children. The oldest child was in the second grade. I went to the funeral home and watched that mother lift those children to look upon the lifeless form of their father in the casket. I wept as I thought of that mother without a husband and those children without a father. But, thank God for the hope of heaven where death and separation will never be known; for heaven will be perfect.

There will be no war in heaven. I was waiting for my plane to return home from a revival meeting. I was near one of our large military bases. I watched service men come and go. I saw them embrace their wives, children and sweethearts. I witnessed their loved ones struggle with their emotions as their husband, son or daughter boarded the plane, not knowing if they would ever see them again. Thank God for the hope of heaven where there will never be another war to be fought; for heaven will be perfect.

There will be no sin in heaven. I've seen children weep over the sins of their parents, and parents weep over the sins of their children. In heaven there will be no alcohol problem, no drug problem and no abuse. There will be no abortion and no perversion. There will be no hate, no bitterness and no revenge. There will be no greed, jealousy or selfishness. There will be no divorce and broken homes. Thank God for the hope of heaven, for heaven will be perfect.

There will be no tempter in heaven. A precious godly man was on his death bed, and Satan was assailing him to the very end. Finally, the dear man lifted his feeble hand and said, "Mr. Devil, I've fought my last battle with you, and I have the victory."

It will be worth every trial, temptation and tear to make it home to heaven. The hardships and heartaches will be past. Every burden will be lifted. Every tear will be dried, and every heartache will be healed. Sorrows will forever be banished. All suffering will be no more. There will be no discouragement, disappointment or death. No complaint will be voiced. No bad attitude will be taken, and no ugly spirit will be manifested. No harsh word will be heard. No more battles will be fought.

Perfect love will abound. We will rejoice with loved ones and the redeemed of all the ages. We will worship and fellowship with our Lord and Savior for all eternity. Heaven will be perfect.

Finally, we note that heaven will be populated. The Hebrew writer declared, "Follow peace with all men, and holiness, without which no man shall see the Lord" (Hebrews 12:14). Dr. Adam Clark said, "To see God is to enjoy Him, and without holiness of heart and life this is impossible. No soul can be fit for heaven that does not have a suitable disposition for the place."

Holiness is the Christian's passport. The Psalmist asked, "Who shall ascend to the hill of the Lord? Or who shall stand in His holy place? He that hath clean hands and a pure heart; who hath not lifted up his soul unto vanity, nor sworn deceitfully" (Psalm 24:3,4).

Anyone that has traveled abroad knows that the one thing you must have is a valid passport. In 1981, I was on my way to the Holy Land. We were in John F. Kennedy Airport in New York, waiting to board our plane for the international flight. They lined us up and were checking passports. There was one man in our group that did not have a valid passport. He had mistakenly picked up a passport that was no longer valid and left his current passport at home. It was a sad moment for he was not able to board the plane and travel with us.

The only passport for heaven is clean hands and a pure heart. It is important that we know our sins forgiven and our hearts cleansed by the precious blood of Christ to be ready for heaven. Holiness is all important.

The seal of the Spirit is essential for heaven. The Apostle Paul wrote in Ephesians 4:30, "Grieve not the Holy Spirit of God, whereby ye are sealed unto the day of redemption." The seal of the Spirit is the witness of the Spirit received in the new birth and entire sanctification. "The Spirit itself beareth witness with our spirit, that we are the children of God: and if children, then heirs; heirs of God, and joint heirs with Christ" (Romans 8:16,17a). God seals His own work and property as evidence that it belongs to Him.

When traveling abroad, each country into which we entered asked to see our passport. After examining it carefully they placed their seal on it, provided that they approved. This meant we were authorized to tour in their country. We must have God's seal, the witness of the Spirit, to be ready for heaven.

The Bible teaches us that election is essential for heaven. "Elect according to the foreknowledge of God the Father, through sanctification of the Spirit, unto obedience and sprinkling of the blood of Jesus Christ" (I Peter 1:2a). The new birth makes us candidates for heaven. Entire sanctification elects us for heaven, provided we continue to walk in the light.

Heart holiness prepares us for the rapture. Paul writes in I Thessalonians 4:16-18, "For the Lord Himself shall descend from heaven with a shout, with the voice of the archangel, and with the trump of God: and the dead in Christ shall rise first: then we which are alive and remain shall be caught up together with them in the clouds, to meet the Lord in the air: and so shall we ever be with the Lord. Wherefore comfort one another with these words." John writes in Revelation 20:6a, "Blessed and holy is he that hath part in the first resurrection."

What about those who are saved and not sanctified should they die before they could get sanctified? Will they be in heaven? May I assure you they are meritoriously atoned for just as a child under the age of accountability, provided they are walking in all the light God has given them. The Apostle John said, "But if we walk in the light, as He is in the light, we have fellowship one with another, and the blood of Jesus Christ His Son cleanseth us from all sin" (I John 1:7). There is both an instantaneous cleansing and a continuous cleansing as we walk in the light.

What about those who have been saved, have light on entire sanctification and have failed to walk in it? Jesus said, "If therefore the light that is in thee be darkness, how great is that darkness!" (Matthew 6:23b). If we fail to walk in the light, we walk in darkness. Light can become darkness, and we can forfeit our relationship with our God and miss heaven.

In Matthew 7:21 Jesus said, "Not everyone that saith unto me, Lord, Lord, shall enter into the kingdom of heaven, but he that doeth the will of my Father which is in heaven."

God's will for every sinner and backslider is to repent. "The Lord is not slack concerning His promise, as some men count slackness; but is longsuffering to us-ward, not willing that any should perish, but that all should come to repentance"
(II Peter 3:9).

God's will for every believer is to be entirely sanctified. Paul wrote to the believers at Thessalonica, "For this is the will of God, even your sanctification, that ye should abstain from fornication" (I Thessalonians 4:3).

The true Church of Jesus Christ is composed of Spirit-filled, holy saints with a Holy Bible their guidebook, the shining highway of holiness their pathway, the Holy Spirit their guide, a holy heart their passport and a holy heaven their destination.

Adam Clark said, "And dost thou not know that holiness and happiness are as inseparable as sin and misery?"

No one goes to heaven by accident. People who go to heaven are people who prepare for heaven. If you are not ready for heaven, you can get ready now. Repent of your sins. Put your faith in the blood of Jesus Christ, and you can be saved. If you are saved, you need to be sanctified. Surrender completely to the will of God in complete consecration. Trust the blood of Christ for cleansing, and you can, by faith, be sanctified wholly. Continue to walk in all the light, and you are heaven bound.

Holiness on Display

Job 1:1-12
"There was a man in the land of Uz, whose name was Job; and that man was perfect and upright, and one that feared God, and eschewed evil" (Job 1:1).

Many deny Divine inspiration in connection with the book of Job. Some claim it to be a novel or work of poetic genius at best. They say that Job never really lived. They want to do away with Job since they claim no one can live as Job lived and still love God and not sin. But God said there was such a man and gives us his name and address.

God has lifted up one man as a world example to demonstrate that holiness will work under any circumstance. He wants us to see that the same grace that enabled Job to stand the test is available to us today.

There are at least four tests that Job faced. The first test was the test of prosperity. His possessions consisted of seven thousand sheep which provided his household with clothes and meat. He had three thousand camels which were the ships of the desert. They took the place of the present day trucks and trains. He had five hundred yoke of oxen which could plow and turn over five hundred furrows of ground at the same time. He had five hundred she asses which provided milk, bore burdens and were a means of transportation. He had much land. If we would allow ten acres for each team of oxen, five thousand acres would be needed for cultivation alone, besides pasture land for the sheep, camels, oxen and asses.

In addition to all these possessions, Job had a very great household, meaning he had many servants. He also had a large family of seven sons and three daughters.

He was a great man with great wealth. He was thought to be a patriarchal chieftain, a desert prince or a king. God said, "... this man was the greatest of all men of the east" (Job 1:3).

Job was wealthy, but he still loved and served God. He feared God in the sense of reverencing, obeying and trusting

God. He put God first in his life and feared lest he would do anything to grieve God He was totally submitted and surrendered to God.

Verse one of chapter one says, "He eschewed evil." Job departed from evil. He avoided and turned away from evil having no desire for it.

The fourth stanza of the song "He Abides" says, "There's no thirsting for the things of the world - they've taken wings; long ago I gave them up, and instantly all my night was turned today, all my burdens rolled away. Now the comforter abides with me."

The good news is that God can save us and sanctify us wholly. He can cleanse our hearts from all sin, and we no longer desire the things of sin and the world. Our great desire is to serve and please our God. We love Him with a perfect love. Self love and world love have been crucified.

Job had holy habits. He worshiped God every day. Daily he offered burnt offerings, early in the morning. He prayed continually for his children lest they had sinned and grieved God.

Three times God said Job was "Perfect and upright" (Job 1:1,8;2:3). He was not absolutely perfect as God is. God is perfect in knowledge, wisdom, power and glory. God is absolutely perfect. Job was not perfect as the angels are for they are an order higher than man and have never been affected by the fall. Job was not perfect as Adam was before the fall. He was not perfect as resurrected, glorified and redeemed saints are perfect. His was a relative perfection, according to the light and revelation God had made available to him in the day in which he lived. The Bible says, "Noah was perfect in his generations" (Genesis 6:9). Noah was judged to be perfect according to the limited light and revelation that he had in the day in which he lived. God did not judge Noah or Job according to the light that He has made available to us in our day. We have much more responsibility because we have received much more truth and Gospel light.

God wants us to experience Christian perfection which is a perfection of love toward God. It does not exempt us from mistakes, errors or the possibility of falling. This perfection is both a crisis and a process. In a moment, we can be made perfect in love. However, there is a never ending process of growth which follows the crisis experience. God is not through with any of us. He wants to develop us more and more into the likeness of His Son, Jesus Christ.

God said Job was perfect and wealthy at the same time. The Apostle Paul said, not money, but, "The love of money is the root of all evil: which while some coveted after, they have erred from the faith, and pierced themselves through with many sorrows" (I Timothy 6:10). Money can indeed be a snare. Paul wrote in I Timothy 6:9, "But they that will be rich fall into temptation and a snare, and into many foolish and hurtful lusts, which drown men in destruction and perdition." Jesus said to His disciples in Matthew 19:23-26, "Verily I say unto you, that a rich man shall hardly enter into the kingdom of heaven. And again I say unto you, it is easier for a camel to go through the eye of a needle, than for a rich man to enter into the kingdom of God. When His disciples heard it, they were exceedingly amazed, saying, Who then can be saved? But Jesus beheld them, and said unto them, with men this is impossible, but with God all things are possible."

Adam Clark said, "It is almost impossible to possess them (riches) without setting the heart on them." However, there have been some that possessed great wealth and did not set their heart on their wealth. R. G. LeTourneau had considerable wealth and gave ninety percent of his income to the work of the Lord while living on ten percent.

Jesus said in Matthew 6:19,20,33, "Lay not up for yourselves treasures upon earth, where moth and rust doth corrupt, and where thieves break through and steal: But lay up for yourselves treasures in heaven, where neither moth or rust doth corrupt, and where thieves do not break through and steal: But seek ye first the kingdom of God, and His righteousness; and all these things shall be added unto you."

Job stood the test. He didn't allow his wealth to come before his God in heaven. He had his priorities right. He kept things in proper balance. God was first.

The second test Job faced was the test of poverty. This is recorded in Job 1:6-22. The sons of God came to present themselves before the Lord. They were high ranking angelic beings and were sons of God by creation. They came to report on their work, to pay homage and for fresh orders. "Satan came also," according to verse six. The Lord said in verse seven, "From whence cometh thou?" Satan answered, "From going to and fro in the earth." Joshua Stauffer said, "Before the fall Satan was evidently head of this solar system, and especially the earth." Since Satan was cast out of heaven, the earth is his field of operation. Jesus recognized Satan as, "The prince of this world" (John 14:30). The Apostle Paul recognized Satan as, "The prince of the power of the air, the spirit that now worketh in the children of disobedience" (Ephesians 2:2). Peter recognized Satan as, "The adversary, the devil, as a roaring lion, walketh about seeking whom he may devour" (I Peter5:8).

God challenges Satan in Job 1:8 saying, "Hast thou considered my servant Job, that there is none like him in the earth, a perfect and upright man, one that feareth God and escheweth evil?" God had confidence in His servant Job. Satan had considered Job much. He tried to wreck his faith through wealth and prosperity, but failed.

Satan accused God of putting a hedge around Job in verses nine and ten. He said, "Doth Job fear God for nought (nothing)? Hast not Thou made an hedge about him, and about his house, and about all that he hath on every side? Thou hast blessed the work of his hands, and his substance is increased in the land." God did not deny that He put a hedge about Job. God does set bounds, and Satan can go no farther than God permits. Paul wrote in I Corinthians 10:13, "There hath no temptation (test, trial) taken you but such as is common to man: but God is faithful, who will not suffer you to be tempted (tested, tried) above that ye are able; but will with the temptation (test, trial) also make a way to escape, that ye may be able to bear it." God knows our frame and will not permit us to be tempted (tested, tried) beyond that we are able to bear.

Satan accused God of making Job his favorite or pet. Satan said in Job 1:10b, "Thou hast blessed the work of his hands, and his substance is increased in the land."

Satan then turned and accused Job of serving God for what he got out of it. Satan said in verse eleven, "But put forth thine hand now, and touch all that he hath, and he will curse thee to Thy face." Satan said Job's righteousness was self-serving.

God gave permission for Satan to touch Job's possessions. However, God restricted Satan. In essence, God said in verse twelve, "He's in your hands, but don't touch Job." Once again we see that Satan can go no farther than God permits.

The calamity breaks on Job as recorded in verses fourteen through nineteen. Satan reveals himself for the ruthless and cruel character that he is. We see him as accuser, thief, liar and murderer.

The first servant comes and reports that the five hundred yoke of oxen were plowing, and the five hundred she asses were grazing. The Sabeans took them and killed all the servants, but the one that came to report to Job.

The second servant comes immediately on the heels of the first servant. He reports that fire, perhaps lightning, burned up the seven thousand sheep, and all the servants, except the one that reported to Job.

The third servant came following the second and reported that the Chaldeans came in three bands, and stole the three thousand camels, and killed all the servants but one. This servant brought the message to Job.

The fourth servant reported that a great wind, possibly a tornado, blew in the eldest son's house and killed all ten of Job's children.

Four terrible blows, one after another. Four symbolizes totality. Job was wiped out. Will Job love God now? God, Satan and men are looking on.

The outcome is recorded in verses twenty through twenty-two. "Job arose, rent his mantle and shaved his head." This was the oriental way of expressing grief. Job fell to the ground as if he had more than he could humanly stand. Job said, "Naked came I out of my mother's womb, and naked shall I return thither: the Lord gave, and Lord hath taken away; blessed be the name of the Lord. In all this Job sinned not, nor charged God foolishly." Job didn't charge God as being unfair or unkind. He stood the test and proved he wasn't serving God for what he got out of it. He had no self-serving intent. He was serving God, because he loved Him.

The third test that Job faced is recorded in Job 2:1-10. Once again there is a council in heaven, and Satan appears. Dr. John R. Church said, "He thought Satan was not anxious for the subject of Job to come up, for he had failed to defeat Job. But, God was proud of His servant, Job, and wanted to talk about him." God said, "Hast thou considered my servant Job, that there is none like him in the earth, a perfect and an upright man, one that feareth God, and escheweth evil? And still he holdeth fast his integrity (perfection or loyalty to God), although thou movedst me against him, to destroy him without cause" (Job 2:3).

Here is the second challenge recorded in chapter two, verses four and five. Satan seemed to feel the previous trial had been unfair. He said to God, "Afflict his body, and he'll curse you to your face." Satan felt that everyone would give up possessions to save his life. He seemed to feel that there was nothing a person would not do to avoid death. God said to Satan, "Behold he is in thine hand; but save his life" (Job 2:6). God expressed confidence in His servant Job. I want to live in such a way that God has confidence in me. God again gave permission with restrictions. Satan could go no further than God allowed.

The second calamity breaks as recorded in Job 2:7,8. Job is smitten with boils, thought to be elephantiasis. It was so named because of the swollen limbs and blackened, rough skin that appeared like that of an elephant. Boils were considered to be a Divine curse. Job expected the disease to be fatal.

The symptoms consisted of severe itching. Job scraped himself with pieces of broken pottery. Another symptom was swelling that caused his countenance to be disfigured. His breath was odorous and drove people away. He said, "My breath is strange (offensive) to my wife" (Job 19:17a). His body was covered with sores that bred worms. Job said, "My flesh is clothed with worms and clods of dust; my skin is broken, and become loathsome" (Job 7:5). Job had restless nights and terrifying dreams. He said, "When I lie down, I say, when shall I arise, and the night be gone? And I am full of tossing to and fro unto the dawning of the day. Then thou scarest me with dreams, and terrifiest me through visions:" (Job 7:4,14). Job could not stand, sit, recline, lie on his face, lie on his back or on his side without extreme pain. His bones burned. He said, "My skin is black upon me, and my bones are burned with heat (my bones burn with fever)" (Job 30:30). He sat among the ashes or the garbage as an outcast. His wife counseled him, "Curse God and die" (Job 2:9). She was saying, "Bid farewell to God. He doesn't love you. If He did, He wouldn't allow this to happen to you." Job replied and said, "Thou speakest as one of the foolish women speaketh" (Job2:10).

God testified of His servant Job and said, "In all this Job did not sin with his lips" (Job 2:10). In all of this terrible ordeal Job did not murmur or complain against God. James said, "If any man offend not in word, the same is a perfect man, and able also to bridle the whole body" (James 3:2). Job stood the test.

Job's fourth test had to do with people and is seen from Job 2:11-37:24. Job's three friends arrive and stare at him for seven days. They weep and express grief and then falsely accuse, misjudge and condemn Job. People can criticize, find fault, and say wrongful and hurtful things that cut deeply. It is so easy to jump on a person when he is down. They accused Job of sin. They believed that righteousness brings material blessings and long life. Since Job had lost everything they concluded that he must be a terribly wicked person. They believed that wicked persons suffer hardship and premature death.

The book of Job refutes the health, wealth and prosperity Gospel that some preach. God's people do suffer material loss, physical affliction and pain.

Horatio Spafford was a successful lawyer in Chicago. He suffered a series of traumatic events in his life. The first was the death of his son. The second was the great Chicago Fire which ruined him financially. He later planned a trip to Europe with his family. Because of business concerns he stayed behind and sent his family ahead. While crossing the Atlantic the ship they were on sank after colliding with another ship. All four of his daughters drowned. His wife survived and sent him a telegram stating, "Saved alone." He later traveled to join his grieving wife. When his ship passed near to where his daughters died, he was inspired to write the words of the hymn, "It Is Well With My Soul." He wrote, "When peace like a river attendeth my way, when sorrow like sea billows roll; whatever my lot, Thou hast taught me to say, It is well, it is well with my soul."

Job revealed human weakness in going through this severe trial. He longed to die. He wished he had never been born. He asked why? Jesus also asked why? He said, "My God, my God, why hast Thou forsaken me?" (Matthew 27:46). The mystery of suffering baffled Job as it has the saints of all the ages.

Job never cursed God or willfully sinned. Even when he could not understand he trusted an all wise loving heavenly Father. He said, "Oh, that I knew where I might find Him! That I might come even to His seat! Behold, I go forward, but He is not there; and backward, but I cannot perceive Him. He hideth Himself on the right hand, that I cannot see Him. But He knoweth the way that I take. When He hath tried me, I shall come forth as gold" (Job 23:3,8,9b,10). He shouted, "Though He slay me yet will I trust Him"(Job 13:15a). He caught a glimpse of the resurrection and said, "I know my redeemer liveth, and that He shall stand at the latter day upon the earth. And though after my skin worms destroy this body, yet in my flesh shall I see God" (Job 19:25,26).

There is a ministry of suffering. God has shouting saints, shining saints and suffering saints. Suffering deepens us spiritually when we take the right attitude. Paul wrote in Philippians 3:10, "That I may know Him and the power of His resurrection, and the fellowship of His sufferings, being made conformable unto His death."

A dear friend thanked God for cancer. Through her experience with cancer she came into a more intimate relationship with her Lord. Through cancer she mined truth from God's Word that she might not have otherwise mined.

Suffering gives God a chance to receive glory. Job's trials have brought God much glory as Christians have been challenged, encouraged and strengthened to endure by the example and victory of Job.

Suffering is a means to our holiness. The Hebrew writer said, "For they verily for a few days chastened us after their own pleasure; but He for our profit, that we might be partakers of His holiness" (Hebrews 12:10). God uses suffering to develop holy character.

Suffering fits us for a ministry of sympathy to others in their suffering. In Hebrews 2:17,18 we read, "Wherefore in all things it behooved Him to be made like unto His brethren, that He might be a merciful and faithful high priest in things pertaining to God, to make reconciliation for the sins of the people. For in that He Himself hath suffered being tempted, He is able to succor (or come to the aid of) them that are tempted (tried or tested)."

Dr. John R. Church was a favorite holiness preacher of mine. He is now in heaven. He had two sons, and both were sickly. Because of what he experienced in the care of his sons God was able to enrich his ministry. He had a sympathetic touch that made him a great blessing to the people to whom he ministered.

Job stood the test and was healed. He prayed for his friends. His possessions were doubled, and his family was restored. Satan was defeated. Job was more than conqueror, and God was glorified.

Job loved God so much that he wanted nothing to do with sin. He shunned it. He turned away from it. Job loved God more than things. Job loved God so much that he would rather die than not to be faithful and true to his God. His wife said, "Curse God." Job said, "That's foolish talk."

Polycarp was a pupil of John, Bishop of Smyrna. In the persecution ordered by the emperor he was arrested and brought before the governor. When offered his freedom if he would curse Christ, he replied, "Eighty and six years have I served Christ and He has done me nothing but good, how then could I curse Him, my Lord and Savior?" He was burned at the stake.

Job did not realize he was on display before the world. All Christians are on display. The world is watching to see how we react under pressure. Will we demonstrate to the world that we love Jesus more than anything and that we are totally surrendered to Him? Will we demonstrate that we love God with all our heart, soul, mind and strength and would rather die than fail Him?

By the grace of God you can stand the test and be true to your God. God wants to display to the world that holiness really works under all circumstances. The chorus says, "I know the Lord will make a way for me; If I live a holy life, shun the wrong and do the right, I know the Lord will make a way for me."

A Man God Can Use

"I sought for a man" (Ezekiel 22:30a)

Dwight L. Moody said, "The world has yet to see what can be done by a man wholly given to God." He further stated, "By the grace of God I will be that man."

Moses was a man God used to deliver Israel from the bondage of Egypt. Joshua was God's man to subdue and conquer the Canaan land. John the Baptist was God's man to announce the coming Messiah. The Apostle Paul was God's man to take the gospel to the Gentiles.

Martin Luther was God's man to declare that man is justified by faith and by faith alone. John Wesley was God's man to declare that we are not only justified by faith, but we are made holy by faith.

William Carey was God's man to pioneer the missionary movement in India. David Livingston was God's man to take the gospel to Africa. Hudson Taylor was God's man to take the light of the gospel to China. The list goes on of those God has used and is using to get the gospel to all the world.

God is still looking for men, women and young people He can use today and until Jesus comes.

How does a person qualify to be used of God? The Apostle Paul tells us of God's tool chest in I Corinthians 1:27-29. "God hath chosen the foolish things of the world to confound the wise; and God hath chosen the weak things of the world to confound the things which are mighty; and base (insignificant) things of the world, and things which are despised, hath God chosen, yea, and things which are not, to bring to nought things that are: That no flesh should glory in His presence." Commissioner Samuel Logan Brengle said, "It's a laughable army! The cross their only weapon! Yes, hidden within their contemptible exterior is the all victorious Christ and the irresistible power of the Holy Ghost."

Who are the people God uses?

First, God uses men and women of purity. He uses people

who have repented of their sins and have been born again. He uses people that have been cleaned up from a life of sin and sinning. The Apostle John wrote, "Whosoever is born of God doth not commit sin; for His seed remaineth in him: and he cannot sin, because he is born of God" (I John 3:9). John tells us that no one can be born of God and continue to live in willful sin. You can't be a Christian and be sinning at the same time any more than you can be sober and be drunk at the same time. The newborn child of God is a new creature or a new creation in Christ Jesus. Paul writes, "Therefore if any man be in Christ, he is a new creature: old things are passed away; behold, all things are become new" (II Corinthians 5:17).

A young father sat on a door step in one of our larger cities. He had been on a drunk and was beginning to get sober. He was dirty, dejected, discouraged and disappointed with himself. Two men from a city mission walked by, saw him and witnessed to him. They told him that Christ loved him, could transform his life and make his life worth living. It sounded good to him. He went to the mission and got gloriously converted. He went home, cleaned up and witnessed to his wife. She saw such a change in her husband and said in her heart, "I want what he has." She went to the mission and got saved. The mother of the young father was a barmaid in the city. She saw such a dramatic change in her son and said, "I like what I see. I don't understand it, but I want what he has." She went to the mission and found the Lord as her personal Savior and quit her job." God was using a young man that had just been cleaned up from a life of sin and sinning.

Jesus called His disciples from their fishing nets, tax collecting and other occupations. They were truly transformed men, and He was using them to preach, heal the sick, cleanse lepers, raise the dead and cast out devils according to Matthew 10:7,8. Jesus commissioned them to preach the Gospel to the world. "He said unto them, go ye into all the world, and preach the gospel to every creature" (Mark 16:15). He was telling them that He wanted to use them in a greater way than ever before, but there was a deeper need in their lives. He said, "Tarry ye in the city of Jerusalem, until ye be endued with power from on high" (Luke 24:49b). "Wait for the promise of the Father, which, saith He, ye have heard of me. For John truly baptized with water; but ye shall be baptized with the Holy Ghost not many days hence" (Acts 1:4b,5).

The promise of the Holy Spirit's fullness involves both cleansing and empowerment. Peter testified in the council in Jerusalem regarding the Jewish Pentecost in Acts 2 and the Gentile Pentecost recorded in Acts 10. He said, "And God, which knoweth the hearts, bare them witness, giving them (the Gentiles) the Holy Ghost, even as He did unto us (the Jews); and put no difference between us and them, purifying their hearts by faith" (Acts 15:8,9). In Acts 1:8 Jesus said, "But ye shall receive power, after that the Holy Ghost is come upon you: and ye shall be witnesses unto me both in Jerusalem, and in all Judea, and in Samaria, and unto the uttermost part of the earth."

The disciples experienced heart cleansing and the empowering of the Holy Spirit in a second work of grace which the Bible calls entire sanctification. It was then that they were mightily used of God.

Peter had been a compromiser. He denied and failed His Lord. Peter immediately humbled himself, repented and experienced forgiveness. Peter went to Pentecost and experienced heart purity and the empowering of the Holy Spirit. It was Peter that preached on the day of Pentecost where three thousand were converted. Pentecost is essential for victorious living and fruitful service. Only sanctified vessels are meet (fit) for the Master's use. We must tarry until our hearts are purified, and we are empowered by the Holy Ghost if we would be used of God.

Sammy Morris was an African boy who was taken from his family and made to be a slave. He was cruelly treated. Miraculously, he escaped and came to the missionaries. They loved him and taught him about Jesus. He was converted and filled with the Spirit. He wanted to know more about the Holy Spirit. The missionary told him he would have to go to New York and meet Stephen Merritt to know more about the Holy Spirit. He started for New York. He was able to join the crew on a ship headed for New York. The men were cruel to him, but in his humble, sweet Christ like way he won many of them to Jesus. When he got to New York he met a homeless man on the dock and asked him to take him to see Stephen Merritt. God had prearranged it, and this man knew where Stephen Merritt's mission was located. Stephen Merritt had to leave and go to a prayer meeting. When he returned Sammy was praying with eighteen men from the streets of New York. Sammy went to Taylor University in Fort Wayne, Indiana. His Spirit-filled life radiated the love of Jesus on the campus and in the churches of the city. The harsh winter climate did not agree with him. He became sick with pneumonia and died. At his funeral several of his school mates volunteered to take the gospel to his people in Africa. Sammy was filled with the spirit and mightily used of God.

God uses men, women and young people who are cleansed from all sin and filled with the empowering presence of the Holy Spirit.

Secondly, God uses men and women of purpose. We read of Daniel that, "Daniel purposed in his heart that he would not defile himself with the portion of the king's meat, nor with the wine which he drank" (Daniel 1:8). He was a teenager in a heathen land. He purposed to be true to His God whatever the cost. He persisted in that purpose throughout his life and influenced men and nations for God.

The Apostle Paul said, "Brethren, I count not myself to have apprehended: but this one thing I do ... I press toward the mark for the prize of the high calling of God in Christ Jesus" (Philippians 3:13a,14).

God uses people who are totally surrendered to Him and determined to do His will at all costs. God's will is not a sideline; it is the main line. God uses those who love Him with all their heart, soul, mind and strength and are purposed to serve Him. They are not seeking fame or fortune. They give of themselves sacrificially because they love Jesus. The Apostle Paul was such a person. I have a medical doctor friend who is on the mission field, living on a missionary's salary, ministering to the physical and spiritual needs of the people.

Why is he doing it? He loves Jesus with all his heart and loves souls for whom Christ died.

God uses people who persevere in spite of discouragement and disappointment. Calvin Coolidge, former president of the United States, said, "Nothing in the world can take the place of persistence. Talent will not; nothing is more common than unsuccessful men of talent. Genius will not take the place of persistence. The world is full of educated derelicts. Persistence and determination alone are omnipotent. The slogan "press on" has solved and always will solve the problems of the human race."

Dr. Lela G. McConnell came to Eastern Kentucky to begin the work of the Kentucky Mountain Holiness Association in 1924. The first winter she was alone and lived in a boarding house in Jackson, Kentucky. She was hungry and cold. The devil tormented her, saying, "You're going to starve and freeze. There won't even be enough money to bury you." Finally, she said, "If I starve or freeze, I'm here until I die." She said, "I heard him (Satan) go, and he never tormented me again like that."

The people God uses don't run when the going gets rough. They stay put. Someone said, "When the going gets tough, the tough get going."

Thirdly, God uses men and women of prayer. E. M. Bounds said, "Not until we prevail with God will we prevail with men." Jesus prevailed in prayer. Again and again He went to a solitary place and poured out His heart to His Father in agonizing prayer. He taught His disciples to pray. In Luke 18:1 we read, "He spake a parable unto them to this end, that men ought always to pray, and not to faint."

Every person greatly used of God has been a man or woman of prayer. Martin Luther said, "If I fail to spend two hours in prayer each morning, the devil gets the victory through the day." John Wesley spent two hours in prayer daily. Bishop Asbury of early Methodism said, "I purpose to rise at four o'clock as often as I can and spend two hours in prayer and meditation." Commissioner Samuel Logan Brengle of the Salvation Army said, "There is no substitute for much wide awake, expectant secret waiting upon God for the outpouring of His Spirit, for gifts of wisdom, strength, courage, hope, faith, discernment of times and spirits, and for a glowing, burning comprehensive message from Him to the people. If any man who would be a soul winner should fail at this point, he will in due time fail at every point."

If you want to be a person God can use, be a person of prayer. An unknown person said, "The devil knows that nothing takes away worldly desires and increases wisdom like prayer. He knows that nothing is so dangerous to his kingdom of darkness as prayer. He knows nothing brings blessing to churches, equips missionaries and ministers (and Sunday school teachers, etc.) more than prayer. Thus, Satan does his best to hinder and destroy our prayer life."

Fourthly, God uses men and women of passion. First, we must have a passion for the Word of God. It is our food, sustenance and strength. The Psalmist said, "How sweet are Thy words unto my taste! yea, sweeter that honey to my mouth!" (Psalm 119:103). God's Word gives us direction. It is our guidebook. In Psalm 119:105 we read, "Thy word is a lamp unto my feet, and a light unto my path." Paul tells us it is Divinely inspired: "All Scripture is given by inspiration of God, and is profitable for doctrine, for reproof, for correction and for instruction in righteousness: that the man of God may be perfect, throughly furnished unto all good works" (II Timothy 3:16). God's Word is mighty in influence. God said, "Is not my word like as a fire? saith the Lord; and like a hammer that breaketh the rock in pieces?" (Jeremiah 23:29). The Hebrew writer says, "For the word of God is quick, and powerful, and sharper than any two-edged sword, piercing even to the dividing asunder of soul and spirit, and of the joints and marrow, and is a discerner of the thoughts and intents of the heart" (Hebrews 4:12).

To be used of God we must have a passion for the Word of God. There is power in God's Word. Paul instructed Timothy, "Preach the Word" (II Timothy 4:2a).

We must also have a passion for a message. Paul said, "I am not ashamed of the Gospel of Christ: for it is the power of God unto salvation to everyone that believeth; to the Jew first, and also to the Greek" (Romans 1:16). Look what the gospel did for the woman at the well. She found water that satisfied her soul thirst, so she would never thirst again. Look what the gospel did for Zaccheus. He was transformed from a dishonest man to an honest man. Look what the gospel did for the Demoniac. "Then they went out to see what was done; and came to Jesus, and found the man, out of whom the devils were departed, sitting at the feet of Jesus, clothed, and in his right mind: and they were afraid" (Luke 8:35).

The message of Scriptural holiness is the message of full deliverance from all sin. It is the message of the empowering presence of the Holy Ghost. We need a passion for this message.

We need a passion for people. Jesus set the example. He had compassion on the multitude. "But when He saw the multitudes, He was moved with compassion on them, because they fainted, and were scattered abroad, as sheep having no shepherd" (Matthew 9:36). He had compassion on two blind men. "and touched their eyes: and immediately their eyes received sight, and they followed Him" (Matthew 20:34b). He had compassion on Jerusalem. He said, "How often would I have gathered thy children together, even as a hen gathereth her chickens under her wings, and ye would not" (Matthew 23:37b). He had compassion on the leper. "He put forth His hand, and touched him, and saith unto him, I will be thou clean" (Mark 1:41b). He had compassion on the bereaved.

"When the Lord saw her (the widow of Nain) He had compassion on her, and said unto her, weep not" (Luke 7:13). He said to her dead son, "Young man, I say unto thee, arise" (Luke 7:14b). Jesus had compassion on the thief on the cross. "Jesus said unto him, verily I say unto thee, today shalt thou be with me in paradise" (Luke 23:43).

Men and women that God uses are men and women of compassion. They have a genuine passion for souls. They weep and work to win the lost and comfort the hurting, suffering and sorrowing.

My mother walked three miles numerous times to visit and pray in the homes of her Sunday school class of boys and girls. She had compassion, and she had a passion for souls.

Finally, God uses men and women who labor in the power of the Holy Spirit. In Zechariah 4:6b we read that it is, "Not by might, nor by power, but by my Spirit, saith the Lord of hosts." God uses people who humbly recognize their nothingness and totally depend on the Holy Spirit. We know that gifts and education are important but are not final in importance. We must wait and seek the Divine touch and anointing upon our labors.

We are but channels through which He works, vessels He must fill, instruments He employs, clay He molds and spending money for Him to spend as He chooses. "It is not ye that speak but the Holy Ghost" (Mark 13:11b). We must have the fresh anointing of the Holy Spirit to be used of God.

The harvest is ripe. Laborers are few. The hour is late and time is short. Who can God use to reap the harvest? God is looking for men and women, young people, boys and girls that He can use. He is looking for people like Isaiah who will say, "Here am I, send me" (Isaiah 6:8b).

Jesus said in Mark 8:35, "For whosoever will save his life shall lose it; but whosoever will lose his life for My sake and the gospel's, the same shall save it."

I had two close friends in school. Both were called to preach. One said, "God has asked me to do too much and is giving me too little in return." He saved his life and lost it. I went to his funeral when he was twenty-nine years of age. He saved his life and lost it.

The other young man surrendered completely to the will of God. He pastored for nearly eight years and then felt the call of God to the mission field. He is still serving the Lord today. He was willing to lose his life for Jesus sake, and he found it in the center of the will of God.

Will you be a man, woman, young person, boy or girl that God can use?